GOD

IS UP TO SOMETHING

GREAT

CAN YOU STAND TO BE BLESSED?

VICTORY LIFE
MEDIA

JERRY BONSU

GOD

IS UP TO SOMETHING

GREAT

CAN YOU STAND TO BE BLESSED?

JERRY BONSU

Published in France by VICTORY LIFE MEDIA an imprint of JBM

JERRY BONSU MINISTRIES
http://www.jerrybonsu.org

VLM books may be ordered through booksellers or by visiting www.jerrybonsu.org. VLM Speakers Bureau provides a wide range of authors for speaking events. To find out more, email us: victorylifemedia@gmail.com

French National Library-in-Publication Data

Dépôt légal: 07/2015

Original and modified cover art by Lali Masriera and CoverDesignStudio.com /Photo by William Djamen

Printed in the United States of America

ISBN: 978-2-9541960-4-6

For further information or permission, contact us on the Internet:

VICTORY LIFE MEDIA "Empowering our Generation for the next Generation" www.victorylifemedia.com.

Dedication

This book is dedicated to all the dreamers and
visionaries who are contributing for the advancement of
God's kingdom in the earth.

CONTENTS

INTRODUCTION

"Life is inevitably filled with trials, and these trials often come on the heels of our greatest successes."

- Anonymous

WE CAN ALL ATTEST to this reality. Life, as we know it, is filled with problems that affect us on many levels. From the relationships that break our hearts to the examinations that strain our brains, life gets more and more challenging with each step of the way. But the greatest lessons in life are often the product of our most serious difficulties.

I don't need to tell you that we live in a world that is filled with doubts and with difficulties, with uncertainties, with frustrations, fear and insecurity. Even those who have put their faith in the cross of Christ can find it difficult to survive in this fallen world where there is bad news after bad news and each day brings another set of problems.

It is truly heartbreaking to watch so many believers losing their faith in the Lord as a result of getting hit with some severe torpedo shots. And unless you have a full understanding as to why God will sometimes allow what we called "bad things" to happen to good people in this life, you can have your personal faith levels in the Lord shaken to its very core depending on the severity of the storm cloud that may have just struck you.

The Scripture tells us that God's people can perish for having lack of knowledge — and not having the right kind of knowledge to fully understand why bad things can even happen to good people in this life, especially to Christians, can cause you to perish in your own personal relationship with the Lord.

Often, many of us face trials and tribulations in life that we do not deal with in a positive light. The stress of our jobs, various family issues, personal relationships, and of course, today's economy, are all critical issues that makes it difficult in overcoming adversity that so many of us are fighting with to resolve our life's battles. Some face severe adversity, while others may not have any serious trials that we would have to overcome. Regardless, how we cope within those moments of crisis determines how we are able to endure and overcome those trying times.

You see, sometimes you must go through the valley to reach the top of the mountain. Figuratively, the valley is what we call the times of adversity. — It is a time of hardship, affliction, recession, depression and otherwise unfortunate circumstances. And we have all had to face it in our lives. If you are like me, you probably thought adversity would never come night your dwelling after you sold out to Jesus. Wow, was I ever wrong!

In the beginning of my Christian walk, it seemed the more I obeyed God the more adversity came my way. I quickly discovered that I didn't like adversity. I still don't. I like peace! But adversity is no respecter of

10

Introduction

persons. All of us will face it. Like a severe storm, you can almost sense it coming, the calm before the storm...

When the storm of adversity comes, it demands your total attention. How you handle them makes all the difference between success and failure. As I always say; "It is one thing to have faith in God, to know that God exists, and that He is all-powerful and that there is nothing that He cannot do or accomplish. But it is quite another thing to be able to fully trust God with your life, and to fully trust Him to properly handle it for you, especially in times of trouble or adversity."

Sometimes life is messy. Just look at Joseph. You might remember the Old Testament story. He was tossed in a pit, wrongfully imprisoned, forgotten, and dismissed. But Joseph's story contains an audacious promise. His life story is one of the most amazing stories of a person's struggle in life that is a textbook example of keeping your faith in times of trouble and overcoming adversity. It shows us how God took what looked like a mess and gave it a message.

The Bible says, Joseph had a dream and his dream was from God. Events in his life caused him to develop his character in adverse situations, but his dream was always with him. From the pit, he ended in the palace (See Genesis 37 to 50).

As children of God, we all take Joseph's Journey. We find ourselves in the pit or in bondage, to things that separate us from God. Only through our

11

commitment to Jesus, and His dream for us, do we find ourselves in the palace.

Brothers and sisters, life is a journey and every one of us is on it. Joseph's journey is our journey. Everything Joseph experienced, we will experience. — Joseph was rejected by his siblings, unfairly imprisoned and lied to by those who could help him. Yet he overcame difficulties and adversity without becoming jaded or bitter.

What kinds of adversities are you facing today? Financial calamity, marriage trouble, hardship from personal attacks, sickness, dream shattered, difficulty in the workplace? Do you believe that God has a plan for your life in spite of the situation and He is up to something great? Listen, whatever mess you face, God will use it for good. He did for Joseph, and He will do it for you.

The Scripture says in Proverbs 3:5-6, "Trust in the Lord with all your heart and lean not on your own understanding; in all your ways submit to him, and he will make your paths straight." Our God is too kind to do anything cruel, too wise to make a mistake, too deep to explain Himself. He said; "I know the plans I have for you," Plans to prosper you and not to harm you, plans to give you hope and a future." (Jeremiah 29:11).

This book is a simple, easy-to-memorize tool based on Joseph's life story to equip you to discover your divine purpose in the midst of adversity. It is intended to help you see how God can turn any mess into a message, any test into a testimony, any trial into a triumph, and any victim into a victor!

Are you eager to get started? So am I. Let's go!

JOSEPH'S STORY;

FROM THE PIT TO THE PALACE

"Now Israel loved Joseph more than all his children, because he was the son of his old age: and he made him a coat of many colours."

Genesis 37:3-4

OF ALL THE BIBLE CHARACTERS, one of my favorite character is Joseph. Next to Jesus, Joseph may be the greatest example of godly character and integrity in the Bible. His life was very interesting and continues to give valuable lessons that are still applicable in our modern times.

Joseph, the favorite son of Jacob, story began with a dream at the age of seventeen. He knew the dreams he was having were from the Lord and that they revealed God's purpose and plans for his life. (See Genesis 37:6-7). In the story, Joseph was always the center of his father's love and attention. Jacob even gave Joseph a colorful coat or garment that came to symbolize how special he was in his father's eyes. Later on, he would pay for his father's actions. Joseph's brothers resented him because he was the favorite son.

Jacob, had two wives, two concubines, and twelve sons.... all competing for his attention. Joseph's family drama have all the makings of a T.V soap opera, with various episodes of jealousy, hatred, deception and self-interest. Reading the account of Joseph's life is like being glued to the T.V screen full of anticipation about what will happen next. Joseph, the dreamer once told his brothers about a dream that a day would come when they would all bow down to him. (See Genesis 37:8, 10-11). This dream made his brothers grow more angry towards him.

One day, Joseph was sent by his father on an errand. Specifically, he was tasked to visit his brothers who were working in the field. The Scripture says that his brothers plotted to kill him but later decided to throw Joseph into a pit. Joseph's brothers also took his colorful coat and wiped it with animal blood. They later lied to their father by saying that Joseph died after being attacked by wild animals. After some time at the bottom of the pit, Joseph was picked up by traveling merchants and later sold him into slavery.

The young lad was later sold by the merchants to Potiphar, one of the Egyptian Pharaoh's trusted leaders. As a worker in Potiphar's household, he became distinguished in his labors. He was later appointed supervisor over Potiphar's household. The story takes a drastic turn when Potiphar's wife falsely accused Joseph of attempting to sexually assault her. Of course, Potiphar's wife did this to get back at Joseph who repeatedly warded off her sexual

16

advances. Enraged by the accusation, Potiphar sent Joseph to prison.

In prison, Joseph again found favor by being able interpret the dreams of the Pharaoh. The Pharaoh was so full of stress and anxiety about the horrible dreams he had and the visions he could not understand. Through Joseph, the Pharaoh was able to understand the economic implications of his dreams for the land of Egypt. Later, he was appointed governor of Egypt. (See Genesis 41).

This remarkable story shows how we, like Joseph, must cling to faith even in the most trying circumstances. Stress and anxiety need not stop us from believing that God has forsaken us and that we have been left alone in the middle of all our troubles. Indeed, overcoming life's challenges is a journey of trust, faith, and perseverance that all of us must take. Like Joseph, we can also dream great dreams and live up to our fullest potential.

Jesus assured us in the book of John chapter 16, verses 33; "I have told you these things, so that in me you may have peace. In this world you will have trouble. But take heart! I have overcome the world." What an amazing statement! Our God is not limited by the natural. All the circumstances might be against us, but He said; "Take heart", "I have overcome the world", "I am still God", "Trust Me. I have got the whole world in My hands." One more day, one more step. I am preparing you for Myself.

In Christ, the "bad things" that happen to us don't break us. Christ uses them to make us. Challenges have always been part of mortality and God's plan for our growth. Growing is a natural process, necessary and important in all areas of life. Plants grow, animals grow, cities grow, children grow, knowledge grows, etc. In the same manner, Christ wants His children to also grow.

No one desires to have a child that does not grow either physically or mentally. Like Joseph, God is preparing us for increase! The story of Joseph is power packed, full of wisdom and truth. I believe every Christian needs to study his story again and again, to help us to trust God, increase in Him, and overcome adversity.

In this book, I have put together 8 major lessons from Joseph (The Dreamer). These revelations have changed me, inspired me, and helped develop character within me. I believe they will do the same for you.

1

JOSEPH HAD A GODLY VISION

"Are You Dreaming God's Dreams for Your Life?"

"But seek first his kingdom and his righteousness, and all these things will be given to you as well."

Matthew 6:33

P. K. BERNARD WAS RIGHT when he said, "A man without a vision is a man without a future. A man without a future will always return to his past." Let's start by clarifying Godly vision. —Management consultants love talking about vision, mission, strategy and so forth. Pastor Chip Ingram in his excellent book Holy Ambition defines vision as "a God-given burden to see what a person, a place, or a situation could become if the grace of God and the power of God were unleashed on them."

Dr. Dick Wynn simply says "Vision is what you see; Mission is what you do." There are many more definitions of vision, and one could carry on discussing this topic for ages. However, for our purposes we will simply define Godly vision as: "The specific plans that God has for my life."

As we read earlier in Jeremiah 29:11, God says, "I know the plans I have for you, plans to prosper you and not to harm you, plans to give you hope and a future." God does have a plan, a vision, a dream for each and every one of His children. Every great accomplishment first begins as a God-given dream in someone's mind. So there is nothing wrong with having vision or dreams for our lives; Dreams for our careers, dreams for our homes, dreams for our ministry, dreams for our community, nation and our generation.

In Ephesians 2:10, the Apostle Paul says:

> *"We are God's handiwork, created in Christ Jesus*
> *to do good works, which God prepared in advance*
> *for us to do."*

It is vital to understand and believe that you are God's workmanship and He has created you for good works. God has already designed what those tasks are to be. And He is the One who enables you to do them. Before you were born, God had a role for you to fill. God created you with a unique blend of talents and passions. You are called to the joy of sharing God's vision for mankind with others, called to be trendsetters in high moral values and conduct, in physical and spiritual integrity. You are called to

22

leadership through service, called to sonship. You are called to be a world changer! You are the Salt of the Earth...the Light of the World! You are not called to make an impression you are called to make an impact!

Now my question is; *"Have you embraced God's Big Vision for your life?"*... One famous Proverb says:

> *"Where there is no vision, the people are unrestrained, but happy is he who keeps the law."*

Proverbs 29:18

You see, without vision you will be outside of God's purpose. Vision is an informed bridge between the present and the future. Without it we perish or go "unrestrained," as the New American Standard Bible puts it. Godly vision is seeing a future reality from God's perspective. It is the capacity to see life and circumstances from God's viewpoint in order to know and to follow God's calling on your life.

True Godly vision gives pain a purpose. It is sanctified dreams. It is the ability to understand what God is saying specifically about you in your life so that you can fulfill the purpose for which He created you and placed you on this planet. A vision from the Lord creates a mission from heaven. Godly vision creates passion in you and that passion motivates you.

As one of my mentor said: "Godly vision is seeing the invisible and making it visible." It is the ability to see with spiritual eyes into a reality that is not apparent to the physical. It is that ability to discover and to discern where you fit in God's overall plan; the direction to go, the passion to pursue, obtaining God's perspective. This is illustrated in the life of Joseph when God gave him two dreams (vision), which told him that he would be a ruler some day.

The Bible says, Joseph believed what the Lord had spoken, and he immediately announced it to his family: "God told me that all of you will bow down to me someday!" Some believe that Joseph made a mistake when he shared this vision, but I believe he was simply excited about hearing from the Lord and shared it in simple faith and humility, not arrogance. However, this bold announcement only served to draw his father's rebuke and feed his brothers' growing hatred. Shortly afterwards, they conspired against him saying, "Here comes that dreamer. Let's kill him! (See Genesis 37:19-21).

A vision from the Lord creates a mission from heaven.

It can be really discouraging when others don't support your dreams (Vision). Joseph brothers hated him yet the more for his dreams, and for his words. Even his father who loves him a lot rebuked him because of that vision he had from the Lord. But he still believed what the Lord had spoken about his future. He now had a purpose for his life even it wasn't received by others.

There are a lot of people who spend their lives living for the approval of others. Too many believers are caught up in looking for "fans," too worried about what others think of them. We are not to be so concerned about who approves or disapproves us, God's approval is what counts. In the next pages, I will share with you about "Dream Killers" and how to keep your dreams alive. Now, let's see why it is so important to have a Godly vision, especially in times of adversity.

—**First**, without the continual revelation of God's Word in your life you cannot maintain spiritual vitality. The Word of God declares:

Man does not live by bread alone, but by every word that continually proceeds from the mouth of the living God.

Matthew 4:4

Most Christians live in timidity, lacking self-confidence, fearful of tomorrow and being insecure about the giants that they now face. They forget their identity in Christ and what the Living Word says about them. The Word of God says: You are more than a conqueror through Jesus Christ who loves you (Romans 8:37). You are the righteousness of God in Christ Jesus (Romans 3:22). You are created in God's image (Genesis 1:27). You are chosen before the foundation of the world (Ephesians 1:4-5). Greater is He who is in you than he who is in the world (1 John 4:4). You have the power to tread upon serpents and scorpions and over all the power of the enemy (Luke

10:19). No weapon formed against you shall prosper (Isaiah 54:17). You really are the head and not the tail, above and not beneath, the rich and not the poor (Deuteronomy 28:12-13). You are created for good works (Ephesians 2:10). You are blessed coming in and blessed going out (Deuteronomy 28:6). You need to remember that you are highly favored of God. Believers who catch a glimpse of the Lord's love for them, His plans for their lives, and His desire to be with them will find confidence and inner assurance that can't be matched.

Above all, remind yourself constantly who the Father says you are and what He thinks of you. Your self-esteem must be based on His opinion, not your analysis or someone else's. It is what God thinks that truly matters. The Scripture makes it very clear in Ephesians 5:17, "Wherefore be ye not unwise, but understanding what the will of the Lord is." If you are not fulfilled in what you are doing or where you are, even if things seem to be going well, don't wait any longer; don't settle for anything less than knowing God's purpose for your life. Ask God to reveal your passions and gifts to you and then use them for His purpose.

—Second, Godly vision quickens faith and zeal to take action and perseverance to sustain the action taken. Show me a zealous person and I will show you someone with vision. While others are waiting around in uncertainty, the one with vision is empowered to take initiative.

26

Throughout history dreamers and visionaries have shaped the destiny of the world. Show two people an empty field and the one without a dream will see an empty field. The dreamer may see a shopping mall, or a tall building, but he will not see an empty field. Dreams are the stuff of which life is made. Dream acts as roadmap on our route to success. It helps in channelling our effort towards a goal.

When dream is in place, future is readily secured. Keep on dreaming for only the dreamers achieve great success in life. Dreamers cause good things to happen, and good just seems to follow and overtake them.

> Godly vision quickens faith and zeal to take action and perseverance to sustain the action taken.

God-given dream is bound to succeed. When a dream is God-given, you can be rest assured, it is a programmed and finished event. The realization of such dream is purely an absolute act of God which can not be hindered nor altered by any mortal man neither the one to whom the dream is given. It is a written and already acted script in the spiritual that only needs to be made manifest in the physical.

Don't miss your appointment with destiny. Be ready! "For the vision is yet for an appointed time, but at the end it shall speak, and not lie: though it tarries, wait for it; because it will surely come, it will not delay." (Habakkuk 2:3).

27

Dream Killers

Can you remember the last time you were telling a friend or family member or even your partner about a dream, a goal you really wanted to achieve? It was probably something you were quite passionate about and talking about it with someone close to you. It got you in high spirits because you could already see it. You could picture yourself opening the door to your new restaurant, clothing store, entertainment agency, etc.

The person you are talking to responds to what you have said, and your energy changes. You are not so excited any more... the vision you had of opening the door to your brand new establishment seems to fade and disappear. Your spirit now feels low, and that disappointed feeling seeps in and your self-esteem drops. If this sounds familiar, know you are not alone. We all have encounters with dream killers.

Joseph's brother saw him coming from afar and said with total contempt, "Behold the dreamer cometh." Dream killers aren't necessarily bad people; neither are they haters. A dream killer could be that good friend, sister, brother, parent who has never really taken a risk on anything because they are terrified of failure. So naturally when you share your God-given dream: establish a new ministry, starting your own business, etc. that would obviously involve taking a risk, they are quick to dissuade you with care. They might say things like: "that will never work", "I

28

don't think you can do it", etc.

In my life I have encountered 2 types of dream killers; the accidental dream killers. They actually care about you, but will unknowingly discourage you from chasing your dreams. There are also, deliberate dream killers (Like Joseph's brothers). They are basically unhappy in their own (most likely) unsuccessful lives, and really don't want to see you progress. Beloved, understand this; not every one will embrace your dream and the earlier you accept it, the more focused you will be.

In the earlier days of my ministry, when God gave me a mandate to "empower and equip individuals through teaching and preaching the uncompromised Word of God, and helping them to fulfill their highest calling and usher them into a supernatural lifestyle of faith and abundant living." Before I knew anything about dream killers and the committee of "they", I wasted valuable time trying to earn the approval of persons I thought were on my side but who were indeed dream killers. That only lengthened the fulfillment of my dream, to my disappointment and made me resentful.

It also made me doubt if I was good enough for the dream. In effect, I doubted God's ability and trust to use me for His glory.

Drawing from the story of Joseph, we see that the dream killer's motive is to terminate our dreams. It is Scriptural truth that the thief comes to steal, kill and destroy (See John 10:10). And a killer is a killer irrespective of what he kills and how he or she does it. He or she is a terminator. Joseph's brothers plan and motive was to stop the birth of his dream even if it meant murdering him.

Dream killers are determined to stop the birth of our vision at whatever cost. But the Bible says that: "When the enemy comes in like a flood, the Spirit of the LORD shall lift up a standard against him." (Isaiah 59:19). God has divinely designed you for a destiny and no one can stop it! Don't let people or fear, intimidation, doubt, lack of finances, etc., dictate to you that you can't fulfill your God-given dream. Talk back to these killers. Tell them, "I can and will fulfill my destiny, my dream in Jesus name!

The Committee of "THEY"

The committee of "they" are those people who have a crab mentality; they have a kind of selfish, short-sighted thinking that runs along the lines of "if I can't have it, neither can you." They rather wish everyone will fail than let themselves fail while others are succeeding.

They represent the "crabs in the bucket" metaphor, where the crabs can easily escape from the bucket, but instead, they grab and pull down each other in a selfish competitive manner which prevents any of them to escape, resulting to their collective demise.

30

The committee of "they" spend most of their time talking about people rather than discussing ideas and solutions. Again, it is because they treat people as their competitors. Understand this, your journey is your journey. You are not in competition with anyone but yourself. Let the negative pressure go. Focus on your own progress and let God lead you to your divine destination. Never let the devil make you doubt who God has called you to be! Don't let anything or anyone convince you against the Word of God. What the Lord speaks with His mouth, His hands will perform.

"Blessed be the Lord the God of Israel, who spoke with his mouth to David my father, and with his own hands hath accomplished it..."

(1 Kings 8:15 DRB)

The world belongs to dreamers. Not pie in the sky dreamers, but dreamers who seek the face of the Lord. God is still in the business of planting great dreams into the hearts of His children. God wants us to achieve and be successful! Yes! He wants us to succeed! He wants us to be full of joy, excited, and full of life! And the committee of "they" would immediately counter and say, "You know brother or sister, it's not God's will for everyone to be successful," but that is not what my Bible says. My Bible says that God wants His children to prosper and be in good health. My Bible says that if we meditate on His Word that we will have success, and that we will prosper.

31

God wants to be the God of champions, not naysayers. He wants us to enjoy all the fruits of the Spirit, all of the time.

Jesus told us that He came that we could have life, and have it more abundantly! He says; we would become like trees planted beside a river of living water, putting forth good fruit that causes not only ourselves, but others to prosper as well.

Beloved, Jesus came that we might have life and have it more abundantly. Don't allow life to drain you. Choose to live an abundant life! Don't let anyone steal your dream. If you have hidden it on the back burner, it is time to place it on the front burner. If fear has stolen your dream, God will place a new dream into your heart.

Don't listen to naysayers, listen to what God has said. He is the number one promise keeper, and if you rely on Him alone and persevere through the trials, you will experience the certainty of His promises.

> Never let the devil make you doubt who God has called you to be!

Joseph's dream was God-given and it certainly came to pass in a wonderful and miraculous way. You need to stand on the promises of God in His Word, despite the circumstances you find yourself in. Do not kill your dream because of the present challenges. Believe in your dream and hold on to God. For the foundation of our Christian faith is the absolute trustworthiness of God's promise that He will protect us and keep us safe, even in the midst of adversity and suffering.

There is no truth which is more generally received than that God is True; but there are few who openly give Him credit for this when they are in adversity. What I want you to understand is that our God is faithful and His grace is always sufficient for us in any and every circumstance of life.

Daniel 11:32 says,

"...but the people that do know their God shall be strong, and do exploits"

Praise God even when you don't understand what He is doing. Praise Him because you know your identity in Christ Jesus. Thank God for all things work together for your good even in the valley. You need not let external circumstance and situations dictate your feelings, behavior, and mindset. Stop believing what others say and start believing what the Word of God says. Until you are willing to accept the authority of God's truth in your life, you will not have the answers you need for the things that trouble your heart and mind.

When you are living your God-ordained purpose no longer are you having to live up to human standards. You become a happier person because external factors and opinions don't get you off track.

You are focused on your path and not anyone else's. The rejection and misunderstanding of others would not matter to you, for in the secret place there is peace!

"For in the time of trouble he shall hide me in his pavilion: in the secret of his tabernacle shall he hide me; he shall set me up upon a rock."

Psalm 27: 5

Living a life of purpose keeps you focused on what God told you to do and not what people think or your present situation. It is when you are focused that you will be blessed. Through His power working in you, your purpose will be fulfilled. And once this happens, you will know because you will begin to feel whole, complete and at peace with whatever it is God has called you to do.

Your God-given dream, or purpose, will inspire you, motivate you, and help restrain your flesh in the absence of any evidence that it is coming to pass. And don't be surprised if some of your fiercest opposition comes from those close to you. Remember, It did for Joseph. —He understood that what God had spoken to him and declared about him was true no matter what the circumstances indicated.

Once you know your vision is from God and you feel peace about it in your heart, then keep talking about it. Never let negative people steal your words or your joy. Words are powerful and it is important to talk about your vision to keep it alive. When you stop

34

talking, then you stop believing; when you stop believing, God can't make it happen because you are no longer operating in faith.

Joseph has never made mistake in telling his brother about his dream, it is purely an absolute act of God. Remember, the Bible says, "All things work together for good to them that love God and are called according to the purpose of God". (See Romans 8:28). So no matter what you are going through, speak the Word! Speak what God says about you in the Scripture! If the Word said you shall have whatever you say, then you shall have whatever you say.

Today, God will take you through a process to help you understand His plan, He will give you discernment and spiritual understanding of what His plan for you is.... Just believe! God is giving you a vision for your life. He is birthing something down in your spirit in Jesus name.

Dream BIG! Talk BIG! And Turn Your Faith Loose!

❖ ❖ ❖

"...Forgetting what is behind and straining toward what is ahead, I press on toward the goal to win the prize for which God has called me heavenward in Christ Jesus

Philippians 3:13-14

Soul Nuggets

1. A man without a vision is a man without a future. A man without a future will always return to his past.
2. God has a vision for your life. He created you with a unique blend of talents and passions.
3. A vision from the Lord creates a mission from heaven.
4. Godly vision quickens faith and zeal to take action and perseverance to sustain the action taken.
5. Living a life of purpose keeps you focused on what God told you to do and not what people think or your present situation.
6. Vision gives pain a purpose.
7. Words are powerful and it is important to talk about your vision to keep it alive.

2

JOSEPH KNEW THAT GOD WAS WITH HIM

"God's Way Isn't Always The Easiest Path"

"When you go through deep waters, I will be with you. When you go through rivers of difficulty, you will not drown. When you walk through the fire of oppression, you will not be burned up; the flames will not consume you. For I am the Lord, your God..."

Isaiah 43:2-3

HAVE YOU EVER HAD A DREAM? Have you ever hoped that things would turn out in a particular way? Have you ever planned for something to happen? Only to find your dreams died, your hopes were dashed and your plans were shattered by circumstances you never thought would happen to you? —Joseph experienced it! He had dreamt of success, of leadership, of influence and of authority but suddenly he found himself tied up on the back of a camel headed for a life of slavery in Egypt. How could he ever trust God again?

How easy it is to trust God when all is flourishing and blossoming with brilliance. But when the troubles come and we are whipped to our knees with no dime in our pocket and no praise on our lips, then trusting God through these times becomes tedious.

I was just 20 years old, idealistic and full of hope when God called me to use my words, through music, writing and speaking, to impact the world. What I didn't know was God's calling on my life would send me on a challenging yet invigorating journey. From the moment I said yes to God, life suddenly got hard. This was shocking. If I was following God's plan and the leading of the Holy Spirit shouldn't pursuing my God-inspired dreams have been easy? —Not exactly.

Our calling was never meant to be easy. It sounds glamorous when we talk about our dreams and all the awe-inspiring things we believe God is birthing out of us: beginning a ministry, starting a business, recording a new worship album or going on a mission trip. Yet, when we find ourselves in the middle of the desert or valley in pursuit of that calling, we can begin to question whether our dreams were actually God-inspired. Even worse, we doubt our ability to keep moving forward to see the calling through to completion.

Most often we tend to think that God has forsaken

us. It is those seasons that shape our lives and build our character. God didn't promise life without storms or challenges. He promised to make us strong to go through those times making us overcomers.

In Isaiah 41:10, the Lord said:

> *" Do not fear, for I am with you; do not be dismayed, for I am your God. I will strengthen you and help you; I will uphold you with my righteous right hand."*

It is not surprising that God repeatedly told Joshua He was with him just before instructing him to lead the Israelites into the Promised Land. That is because being called by God can feel like a moment of isolation. When we pursue God's plan, well-meaning people will not always understand our specific calling, and that may cause some people (even friends) to turn away.

It is true that God's calling can set us apart, whether for a moment or an extended season, but He never intended for us to do it alone. He also confirmed this to us in the book of Hebrews, verses 13, "Never will I leave you; never will I forsake you."

These two unequivocal and absolute statements in the book of Isaiah and Hebrews carries us

> Do not fear, for I am with you; do not be dismayed, for I am your God.

through the darkness of life and give us assurance that God is our supernatural parent Who watches over us. Because we are His creation, He promises to give us the grace to sustain all things. It is a constant that is there forever. We may be persecuted, but we will not be abandoned, we may be struck down, but not destroyed. Just as God promised Joshua to never leave him nor forsake him, so it is with us.

We have been given the promise of the Holy Spirit, who is not only with us, but also within us. God's Spirit leads, comforts, directs, instructs and testifies that we are inheritors of the Kingdom. If there are moments on your journey that you feel isolated while fulfilling God's calling, remember you have the power of the Holy Spirit in you and with you. The love of God that is in you is greater than any circumstance!

In Romans 5:5, the Bible declares:

"And this hope will not lead to disappointment. For we know how dearly God loves us, because he has given us the Holy Spirit to fill our hearts with his love."

Beloved, regardless of how things look around you, know that you are not alone. The Greater One lives within you. You are never in a less than position because of God's favor, love, and anointing He has so richly given to you. Never doubt the love and the goodness of God to you. He doesn't promise a storm free life but He does promise to be the anchor in the storm so that you will not be overcome! Trust Him daily. Trust Him hourly and learn to trust Him moment by moment. His resources will not only get you through but you will truly grow to experience Him as the source of hope overflowing by the power of the Holy Spirit.

HE BROUGHT US OUT TO BRING US IN

In Deuteronomy 6:23, the Bible says: "And He brought us out from there, that He might bring us in to give us the land which He swore to give our fathers." In other words God did not save you and me from sin to leave us with the shame and wounds of our past. He brought us out to bring us into the freedom, liberty and prosperity of Christ... into the good plan He has for our lives.

In order for us to walk in the plans God has for us, we need to go through times of transition, which can sometimes be painful. Transition is the place we go through when we are coming out of something and heading into something else. It could be the best experience, or the worst experience.

I have gone through many transitions in my life. Through them all, God has brought me to the place where I can share my testimony and help others. But when I was going through those things, it was not an enjoyable experience. Many times I was confused and miserable, and I didn't understand what was going on.

43

I felt like giving up every few minutes. Praise God He was working through it all to accomplish His purpose for my life!

Often it takes silence and separation to transition into your next season. When we are going through transition, we usually want our circumstances to be different; we want relief from the pressure. But many of our circumstances don't change when we want them to because God is using them to change us. The truth is, God will sometimes allow us to be in a place of need and have problems we can't solve. Why? Because, like it or not, "Need" drives us to seek Him. —It is easy to quote Bible verses when things are going well, but it is another thing to really live by them when we are in the midst of difficult circumstances.

> We may be persecuted, but we will not be abandoned, we may be struck down, but not destroyed.

God doesn't want to be there for us only in times of trouble; He wants us to seek Him in the good times as well as the hard times. God wants His people to get to the place where we know that we need His presence and guidance at all times. Then, even after He brings us out of the wilderness and into a time of blessing in our lives, we won't forget how much we need Him.

Another major change God is seeking to accomplish in us during times of transition is learning how not to live by our feelings but to live by faith in His Word. You and I need to be determined to endure all the way through and not give up no matter how we feel.

God is our mighty bulwark during times of pain, sorrow, lack of money, betrayal, or whatever life brings, for He is the anchor promised to us. And so, in times of great fear when enemies paralyze and numb the spirit just remember what God said in the book Deuteronomy 31:6,

> *"Be strong and courageous. Do not be afraid or terrified because of them, for the Lord your God goes with you; he will never leave you nor forsake you."*

Praise God! Some of the things fighting you are simply preparing you for where you are going!

Sometimes God let you go through the wilderness first, so when you get ready to lead others, you will have credibility through the things you have suffered. Today, whatever you have lost in your life, get ready because God is about to restore it. See the things that are ahead. Set your eyes upon those things and let His Word be your strength. And hold on to the promises. You are being prepared for the things ahead, with the opportunities of the present giving you a "taste" and a "sip" of what is ahead.

Rejoice! Because the Lord is standing with you now and He is turning it around for you! Even though it may not "feel" like it, or "look" like it, believe that Jehovah Sabaoth, THE LORD OF HOSTS is standing with you and strengthening you. He is delivering you out of the enemy's mouth! Keep resisting and stand! You are being perfected and completed —an eternal purpose!

Here is the Apostle Peter's advice: *"...put away all pride from yourselves. You are standing under the powerful hand of God. At the right time He will lift you up. Give all your worries to Him because He cares for you. Keep awake! Watch at all times. The devil is working against you. He is walking around like a hungry lion with his mouth open. He is looking for someone to eat. Stand against him and be strong in your faith. Remember, other Christians over all the world are suffering the same as you are. After you have suffered for awhile, God Himself will make you perfect. He will keep you in the right way. He will give you strength. He is the God of all loving-favor and has called you through Christ Jesus to share His shining-greatness forever."*

1 Peter 5:6-10 (NLV)

Some of the things fighting you are simply preparing you for where you are going!

The Psalmist also encourages us to hope in God and know that He is with us. He says: "God is our shelter and strength, always ready to help in times of trouble. So we will not be afraid, even if the earth is shaken and mountains fall into the ocean depths; even if the seas roar and rage, and the hills are shaken by the violence. There is a river that brings joy to the city of God, to the sacred house of the Most High. God is in that city, and it will never be destroyed; at early dawn He will come to its aid. Nations are terrified, kingdoms are shaken; God thunders, and the earth dissolves. The Lord Almighty is with us; the God of Jacob is our refuge. Come and see what the Lord has done. See what amazing things He has done on earth. He stops wars all over the world; He breaks bows, destroys spears, and sets shields on fire. "Stop fighting," He says, "and know that I am God, supreme among the nations, supreme over the world." The Lord Almighty is with us; the God of Jacob is our refuge." (Psalm 46:1-11 NLT).

Wow! Isn't it wonderful to know that God is with us every day and always ready to help in times of trouble? I don't know how big the storm is, but whatever you are facing today, God loves you enough to allow you to go through these times to be able to face what is ahead. He is increasing your platform to impart the anointing and faith that you have received during these times. The Lord is placing His Hands into the soil of your life to break up the fallow ground. Like a skilled farmer, He is tilling and turning the ground beneath your feet. There are so many that need that which you are receiving during this season. So don't let the season of preparation discourage you or dampen your faith. Don't let it obscure your vision.

Hang on! The seasons are changing. The winter season is coming to a close. Fresh spring rains are on the way. Times of refreshing and new life are quickly approaching. God is about to visit you in the coming days with an unprecedented outpouring. Discern the transition, and position yourself correctly in the midst of it. Surrender to that inward pull to come back to place of private prayer, devotion and holiness. Fall on your knees, and experience the clarity of God's voice and the sweetness of His presence.

Beloved, don't let what you see dictate what you believe. Walk by faith not by sight! Joseph refused to let his circumstances shape his outlook. He allowed no self-pity or bitterness to rob him of energy. Instead, he chose to use each circumstance — whether at home, at Potiphar's house, or in prison as God's appointed place where he would serve Him with all of his heart. Instead of using the delayed promise as a reason to grumble against God, he kept it in the back of his mind to give him courage and strength. He let go of expectations of how and when God would carry out the promise.

In fact, Joseph knew that the same God who brought him out of the pit is with him, and He will make way out of no way. In the meantime God was up to something much bigger than he could have imagined. Just because God seems silent doesn't mean you should doubt Him or stop praying. God's silence isn't a license for us to turn our backs on Him. Instead, it is an invitation to press forward and seek Him even more diligently.

The God that we serve is not human, that He should lie, not a human being, that He should change His mind. Does He speak and then not act? Does He promise and not fulfill? (See Numbers 23:19). God is a God of order. He does everything by appointment. He has a set appointment to bring to pass His promise in your life. He said: "For the vision (revelation) is yet for an appointed time, but at the end it shall speak and not lie; though it tarry, wait for it because it will surely come; wait for it." (Habakkuk 2:3 JUB).

Friend, God didn't bring you this far to leave you! He didn't bring you this far for nothing. His thoughts and Words are always in perfect alignment. Know that whatever He has spoken concerning your life will surely come to pass because He watches over His Word to perform it! Nothing the enemy tries will change the plan of God for your life! Even if your circumstances contradict your purpose...... your purpose will always prevail! It is the opposition that shows us that God is working. So stand firm on God's promise and trust God's process... it may be uncomfortable, it may hurt, it may humble you, it may push you to your limits, but He won't lead you astray!

❖ ❖ ❖

"Trust in the Lord with all of your heart; do not depend on your own understanding. Seek his will in all you do, and he will show you which path to take."

PROVERBS 3:5-6

Soul Nuggets

1. God didn't promise life without storms or challenges. He promised to make us strong to go through those times making us overcomers.
2. Just as God promised Joshua to never leave him nor forsake him, so it is with us.
3. God's Spirit leads, comforts, directs, instructs and testifies that we are inheritors of the Kingdom.
4. Often, it takes silence and separation to transition into your next season.
5. Be strong and courageous.
6. Don't let what you see dictate what you believe. Walk by faith not by sight.
7. God let you go through the wilderness first, so when you get ready to lead others, you will have credibility through the things you have suffered.
8. See the things that are ahead. Set your eyes upon those things and let His Word be your strength. And hold on to the promises.

3

JOSEPH WAS FAVORED BY GOD

"Let God Promote You"

"When his master saw that the Lord was with him and that the Lord gave him success in everything he did, Joseph found favor in his eyes and became his attendant. Potiphar put him in charge of his household, and he entrusted to his care everything he owned."

Genesis 39:3–4

GRACE IS OFTEN IDENTIFIED as unmerited or underserved favor. Favor, however, can have a broader definition, as favor can be released upon a person for obedience, hard work, or acts of kindness. Favor is God's "I'm for you" attitude. It is the amazing, undeserved benefit of being His child, yet many believers never tap into its fullness. —Why? One reason is that we simply misunderstand God's favor.

The Bible declares in Psalm 8:5, that God has crowned us with glory and honor. That word here honor translated as favor, and favor means to assist, to give you special advantages and to receive special treatment.

Biblically, favor can also be defined as "tangible evidence that a person has the approval of the Lord." It is the friendly disposition from which kindly acts proceed to assist, to provide with special advantages, to receive preferential treatment. That is God's heart toward us. He wants to bless, help and promote us. He wants to treat us special.

When we favor someone, we want to be with him or her. We delight in him. We connect with her in a way we don't connect with everyone. We usually favor people who also favor us. In the same way, God shows favor to the ones who delight in, connect with, and give honor to Him.

He says in Isaiah 66:2:

"My hands have made both heaven and earth; they and everything in them are mine. I, the Lord, have spoken! I will bless those who have humble and contrite hearts, who tremble at my word."

God never intended His favor to be found by just a handful of people. Every believer, you and I included can find His favor and do things that could not be accomplished without it. Sometimes it is difficult for us to comprehend in our limited minds how God masterfully orchestrates our lives with seasons of blessing and access that we do not deserve and cannot earn. Yet favor abounds!

The favor of God isn't about having more money or easier circumstances. It is about enjoying the kindness of God, sovereignly, yet freely offered to all who will receive Jesus Christ and the life He has to offer.

God favor is not for a season but for a lifetime. It is the current that moves you from your present situation into the destiny that God has for you. It puts you in the right place at the right time to meet the right person to unlock your destiny! God's favor will do for you what your education, your spouse, your personality, your abilities, and your career cannot do. This divine favor takes you from ordinary to extraordinary! The Bible records numerous examples of God's favor upon His people causing them to experience many breakthroughs.

> God shows favor to the ones who delight in, connect with, and give honor to Him.

When Joseph was falsely accused of seducing his boss's wife, he was sent to prison. While in prison, "The Lord was with Joseph and showed him mercy and gave him favor in the sight of the keeper of the prison" (Genesis 39:21). Joseph was so highly favored that the head of the prison gave Joseph the authority over all the prisoners, and did not "look over Joseph's shoulder" to check out his faithfulness (See Genesis 39:23).

This story reveals a dynamic truth. God's favor produce Supernatural increase and promotion indeed! It makes ordinary students shine in an extraordinary way. It makes lonely singles attractive, married people desirable to their spouse, employers gain influence, employees receive recognition, entrepreneurs attract contacts. It is a magnet to the blessing and promotion of God.

In fact, when the favor of God envelops you, you cease to labor in vain. It brings divine acceleration in your advancement. It release great blessings, including; prosperity, health, protection, favor, peace, increase, opportunity and advancement. These come as a result of God's grace towards us.

However, favor is always attached to a purpose and comes with a price. When favor comes, trials and tribulations also come. Favor doesn't mean always bed of roses but both blessings and tribulations are part of it. It brings challenges in life. As Laetitia (My wife) said; "The next level will bring new friends, new enemies, new challenges, new favor, and new opportunities!" It is no small thing to be highly favored by God. Especially when you are acutely aware of how preposterous this idea truly is.

To know that you are favored by God can be a life-changing moment. It is the kind of thing that changes your perspective on the world. I remember when I realized that I was highly favored by God. It didn't come to me an instant. It was something I realized over time, and when it finally struck me, it changed my world. When you realize that you are highly favored by God, nothing will ever be the same.

In the story of Joseph there are some things that cannot be denied, because the Scripture makes it clear that: Joseph was chosen and anointed by God. He had a destiny given by God. He was favored by God, and also by his earthly father (Jacob). God was with him.

That sounds like a winning combination, judging from that criteria it would look like Joseph had it made. But when we read the Scripture we find out that this same Joseph who had everything going for him, who was anointed by God, who was favored by his father and had so many great advantages; One day found himself in a pit.

If you have ever been in the pit, I don't have to tell you what it is like. The sense of hopelessness or utter despair can be so powerful it is easy to believe there is no way out. Whether it be from the pain of rejection, the sting of betrayal, loneliness in your marriage, the ache of an addiction, or even the loss of a job or dream, we can begin sinking down into a dark, slimy pit and before long we are wondering if we will ever be able to crawl back out.

I don't know what that pit is for you today: It may be a pit of debt. It may be a pit of sickness. It may be a pit of bondage, or addiction. It may be a pit of depression. It may be a pit of marriage problems that looks so deep and so dark and impossible that you feel like giving up. It may be a spiritual pit and you just don't feel God like you used to, and you are dry and discouraged. But always remember no pit is impenetrable to a God who specializes in pulling people from the slimiest of pits. Your present condition or your surroundings have no bearing on God's ability to bring favor into your life.

I declare and decree that you are coming out of the pit right now in Jesus name! Because of God's favor that surrounds you as with a shield, you will not die in the pit! Instead, you will live to tell what the Lord has done.

> God's favor produce Supernatural increase and promotion!

Wherever you are today; "The Lord make his face shine on you and be gracious to you; the Lord turn his face toward you and give you peace." (See Numbers 6:25-26). I decree and declare that you will see Ephesians 3:20, exceedingly, abundantly, above and beyond favor and increase in every area of your life.

From today, no limits! No boundaries! I see nothing but favor and increase all around you! God is about to turn it around for you! I don't know how He is going to do it. I don't know when He is going to do it. I don't know who He is going to use to do it. But I know one thing the pit is not your final destination!

Repeat this after me: I see my increase and abundance! I flow in the Supernatural of God! I flourish in Divine Favor in Jesus mighty name. Amen!

Favor, Your Supernatural Ladder
To Promotion

Beloved, do you realize the favor of God on your life actually has a purpose? This purpose is beyond your physical limitations. God's favor transcends geography, inheritance and most importantly takes you beyond your talents.

Joseph was a dreamer, but the dreams were not enough. Joseph needed the favor of God to propel him into his destiny, a destiny that was way beyond the geographic location of Joseph (on his father's land in Israel). This favor was beyond the physical abilities that Joseph had (a big mouth). It was also beyond the evil plans of his brothers and Mrs Potiphar's false accusation. It is the favor of God that propelled him into his destiny, thereby fulfilling God's perfect will for him.

"For promotion cometh neither from the east, nor from the west, nor from the south. It is God who judges: He brings one down, He exalts another."

Psalm 75:6

From today, no limits! No boundaries! I see nothing but favor and increase all around you!

The Bible says that promotion comes from God. And He is the Judge. In other words, God is the One who decides who gets promoted, when they get promoted, how they get promoted, and where they get promoted. Also the Scripture says; exaltation comes from Him alone! I believe that we are in a season where God wants to elevate His children and promote us. Promotion is coming to our lives in a radical way!

Without a doubt, I believe God has a purpose and destiny for each of every one of us and He wants us to enter into it. He wants to lead His children in the pathway of promotion.

Often we may go through the path of trials and tribulations in order to be shaped and refined and prepared to enter into the destiny that God has prepared for us. God leads us through a process of shaking and discipline which can be painful at that times, but later it will prove to be the greatest thing that could have ever happened to us. Why? Because it is the process that was needed to get us to our promotion.

> God is the One who decides who gets promoted, when they get promoted, how they get promoted, and where they get promoted.

Unfortunately, a lot of people want the promises of God (The promotion) without the process. It won't happen! God will not allow the unprepared to see new opportunities. God's promise is always on the other side of the process. In order to deliver what God put in you, you have to endure the pain of this moment. In fact, the promise is in your pain. The Promise is in

60

your discomfort. The Promise is in your ability to strengthen yourself and trusting God!

Brothers and sisters, peace comes from trusting God, and from trusting the process. God won't allow things in your life that He can't bring you out of and use for your advantage. "If we endure hardship, we will reign with Him." (See 2 Timothy 2:12)

As a matter of fact, the only way you could avoid the process is if it is man that is promoting. The painful reality about being promoted by man is that man operates according to his feelings. He will put you up today and cast you down tomorrow. Because true promotion only comes from God, not man!

If God promote you, He promotes you so that He could receive the glory from your life. Now, it is up to you to determine if you are promoted into that plan or not. Your willful obedience to what God is trying to do in and through you, determines if you are promoted or not. God wants to take you from where you are to where He wants you to be! For God knows the outcome before He even begin!

"I knew you before I formed you in your mother's womb. Before you were born I set you apart and appointed you as my prophet to the nations."

Jeremiah 1:5 (NLT)

In other words, God is declaring to you and I, "I promoted you before you were born." Yes, God

GOD IS UP TO SOMETHING GREAT

foreknew us and He has a plan for us too, plans to prosper us, plans to give us hope and a future. Just like Abraham, Joseph, David, Esther, Job, Daniel and Jeremiah. It does not matter where we are in life, who we are, what our condition may currently be, God can and will promote us.

We all need to become favor-minded. That is, we must become conscious of God's desire to bestow His divine favor upon us. Think about that! God wants to give you special privileges. He wants you to walk into His blessings. He said in Isaiah 49:8, "In the time of my favor I will answer you, and in the day of salvation I will help you; I will keep you and will make you to be a covenant for the people, to restore the land and to reassign its desolate inheritances," Once again, understand that God's favor is open to all, to anyone who opens up freely to the son of man, Jesus. -

True promotion only comes from God, not man!

—He is the surest way to divine promotion!

Because of His sacrifice, we can walk each day in power, wholeness, purpose and life. The Scripture says we should walk in God's love and favor! — Walking in God's favor takes you to new heights and places you never thought you could reach without God! I pray that God's favor may speak for you, and accelerate your progress in all you do in Jesus' name.

Friend, when God gives favor; people favor you, and often for no reason they can even explain. Favor is actually a part of grace. In the English New testament, the Word 'grace' and the word 'Favor' are both translated from the same word "Charis". So the grace of God is the favor of God. And the favor of God is the grace of God; that which causes things to happen in our life that need to happen through the channel of faith. In this season of your life God's power is doing something for you that you can neither earn nor deserve.

Today, I boldly declare that; "The hand of God is shifting you to a new level of your destiny. So get ready! A new season of joy is rapidly coming upon you. God's Presence is all over you in Jesus Name! His favor is making a new way for you now." No matter what is going on in your life, get your expectancy up. Be on the lookout for God's goodness because a flood of favor is coming your way! Today believe that you are blessed and highly favored by God! And remember, trusting and having faith in the Lord is the key to God's kingdom.

I pray that God's favor cause people to go out of their way to bless you without even knowing why they are doing it. May the favor of the Lord our God rest upon you; establish the work of your hands for you in the mighty name of Jesus!

NOW repeat this after me:

"Dear God, I seek Your favor upon my life today. Because You have given me Your righteousness, I believe that I have found favor in Your eyes. Because You are a covenant-

keeping GOD, You will look on me with favor and make me fruitful and bring increase in my life. Like Joseph, I will prosper in every position, concern, or situation where I am in, because the Lord is with me. Because of Your favor, I experience preferential treatment from other people. Since I work with integrity I will obtain favor from You. Your Word says, a good man obtains favor from the Lord, and those who do what is right cannot be removed. I actively seek and live by Your higher wisdom; therefore, I am highly favored and esteemed in the sight of God and men. Your favor brings promotion and approval. You O Lord take pleasure in my prosperity. You desire for me to prosper in every area of my life — spiritually, financially, emotionally, physically, mentally and socially. You surround and protect me with favor like a shield; therefore, no sickness or disease can live in my body. I thank You Lord that Your favor upon my life endures for a lifetime. I give You praise and honor. In Jesus' name, Amen!"

This is what the Lord says:

❖ ❖ ❖

"I will look on you with favor and make you fruitful and increase your numbers, and I will keep my covenant with you."

Leviticus 26:9

BENEFITS OF WALKING IN THE FAVOR OF GOD

- **Supernatural increase and promotion**
  (Genesis 39:20b-22)
- **Provision and overflowing harvest**
  (Deuteronomy 33:16)
- **Restoration of every lost thing**
  (Exodus 3:21, Job 33:26)
- **Prominence and preferential treatment**
  (Esther 2:17)
- **Divine Protection**
  (Psalm 5:11-12)
- **Honor even in midst of adversaries**
  (Psalm 5:11-12)
- **Divine Increase**
  (Deuteronomy 33:23)
- **Prayers are heard and answered**
  (Psalm 69:13, 84:11)
- **Divine Intervention**
  (Psalm 44:3)

Soul Nuggets

1. True promotion only comes from God, not man!
2. When you realize that you are highly favored by God, nothing will ever be the same.
3. Your present condition or your surroundings have no bearing on God's ability to bring favor into your life.
4. God's favor transcends geography, inheritance and most importantly takes you beyond your talents.
5. The favor of God isn't about having more money or easier circumstances. It is about enjoying the kindness of God, sovereignly, yet freely offered to all who will receive Jesus Christ and the life He has to offer.
6. God shows favor to the ones who delight in, connect with, and give honor to Him.
7. When God gives favor; people favor you, and often for no reason they can even explain.
8. Favor, however, is always attached to a purpose and comes with a price.

4

JOSEPH
MAINTAINED HIS INTEGRITY

"Can You Stand To Be Blessed?"

"But he refused and said to his master's wife, "Look, my master does not know what is with me in the house, and he has committed all that he has to my hand. There is no one greater in this house than I, nor has he kept back anything from me but you, because you are his wife. How then can I do this great wickedness, and sin against God?"

Genesis 39:8-9

INTEGRITY. WE HEAR THIS WORD mentioned a lot, especially as Christians. But, exactly, what is it and how do we live with it? If you were to look up the word "integrity" in the dictionary you would find definitions like: "The quality of being honest and having strong moral principles; moral uprightness. — truthfulness, honesty, wholeness, entireness, without deceit or corruption." But for those of us who are

Christians; followers of Christ, integrity means much more: Is to live my life by godly standards, godly principles and godly values, no matter where I am, who I am with or what my circumstances may be.

Integrity glorifies God, protects us from stumbling, and encourages growth. It reflects godly wisdom. From the beginning of human history satan has tried to confuse and confound God's purposes by corrupting man's thinking. In the Garden of Eden he succeeded by calling God's character into question and convincing Eve that her disobedience would have no consequences. To this day he continues to deceive entire civilizations by blinding the minds of the unbelieving, that they might not see the light of the gospel of the glory of Christ. The Bible says:

The god of this age has blinded the minds of unbelievers, so that they cannot see the light of the gospel that displays the glory of Christ, who is the image of God.

2 Corinthians 4:4

We live in a time where integrity means nothing. Today it is difficult to tell the good person from the bad person. satan is constantly seeking to break our integrity. When leaders, parents, friends, pastors, etc. fail to maintain integrity, their relationship, nation, family, ministry, and even the work of the Church suffer the consequences. Christians are called to be holy and live a life of purity. The apostle Paul believed that true Christian loyalty can be very strong. He wrote: "I am convinced that neither death nor life... nor things now here nor things to come... nor any other creation will be able to separate us from God's love that is in Christ Jesus our Lord." (See Romans 8:38, 39). We can have a similar conviction if our love for God is strong. Such love is an indestructible bond that not even death can conquer.

Jesus models integrity by living a whole and integrated life in which His inner life (intimate relationship with the Father) and outer life (the life the world saw) were consistent. God desires that we be whole or complete in Christ. So that our beliefs, attitudes, words, and actions consistent with His nature. He looks for men and women of integrity who live holy lives that are accountable to Him and to the Body of Christ.

In the Bible, there are three senior public servants mentioned who attained their position in a foreign country and demonstrated that you can be successful without compromising your faith and integrity. They are Nehemiah, Daniel and Joseph. From **Nehemiah** we learn his achievement in building the walls of Jerusalem and more importantly rebuilding the community of God's people after the exile.

From **Daniel** we learn his ability to serve different four kings, in three different empires; for it matters not who the civil authority may be when God is on the throne of your heart! And then we come to **Joseph**. As we read, Joseph was favored by his father Jacob over all his brothers.

71

Let's take a quick look at Joseph and the godly character that he exhibited; and at how it is desperately needed today in our Christian lives.

In Genesis 39, we see that Joseph is put in charge of Potiphar's household. Because of his godly character and integrity, he has found favor with Potiphar. Joseph's positive attitude speaks volumes to Potiphar, and probably every one in his household also. He trusts Joseph with everything he owns. Yes, Potiphar placed everything he owned into Joseph's care!

> Integrity glorifies God, protects us from stumbling, and encourages growth.

Joseph's character was such that Potiphar did not concern himself with anything but the food he ate. The Scripture says:

"And Joseph found grace in his sight, and he served him: and he made him overseer over his house, and all that he had he put into his hand. And it came to pass from the time that he had made him overseer in his house, and over all that he had, that the LORD blessed the Egyptian's house for Joseph's sake; and the blessing of the LORD was upon all that he had in the house, and in the field. And he left all that he had in Joseph's hand; and he knew not ought he had, save the bread which he did eat. And Joseph was a goodly person, and well favoured."

Genesis 39:4-6

72

True character and integrity puts a person in the position to be trusted to the point that they do not need constant supervision. We can see from the above verses that Potiphar gave Joseph complete administrative responsibility over everything he owned. With Joseph there, he didn't worry about a thing, except what kind of food to eat!

Friend, how you live reveals the core of who you are. Your actions flow from your inner motivation. Integrity has to do with the consistency of what you do with who you claim to be. While there are those that say that it is difficult to maintain personal integrity in a different culture with a different value system, the clearest example of Joseph's integrity was when he was tempted by Potiphar's wife.

"And it came to pass after these things that his master's wife cast longing eyes on Joseph, and she said, "Lie with me."

Genesis 39:7

Consider Joseph's situation, bought as a slave by Potiphar. He was elevated to the top of the household. But then his master's wife attempts to seduce him. A man of lesser character would have given in. But Joseph would rather go to prison than to betray his master and his integrity. Note his response to Potiphar's wife in Genesis 39:9, "There is no one greater in this house than I, nor has he kept back anything from me but you, because you are his wife.

How then can I do this great wickedness, and sin against God?" Joseph knew that if he gave into the temptation, he would betray not only his master but more importantly his God. Joseph knew that even if Potiphar, or anyone else never found out, God knew and he would not commit such a horrible sin before God.

> **How you live reveals the core of who you are.**

Believe it or not the time will come when you too will be forced to make a decision concerning your personal integrity. Joseph teaches us that integrity means not compromising God's standards. It does what is right even when every one else is doing wrong. God held such a high position in the heart of Joseph, and because he honored God, he would honor Potiphar. Even when the situation was such that no one else would know.

Our magnificent Creator God knows everything and He is the source of all true knowledge, understanding, and wisdom. His knowledge is undefiled by any distortions or wrong perspectives. It is totally true and accurate. God knows the answers to all of life's questions. Unlike us, God is never surprised or bewildered because He is always completely aware of all events past, present, and future. He also knows everything about us; our desires, motives, and thoughts. God knows more about us than we will ever know about ourselves. King David writes; "O Lord, You have examined my heart and know everything

74

about me. You know when I sit down or stand up. You know my every thought when far away. You chart the path ahead of me and tell me where to stop and rest. Every moment You know where I am. You know what I am going to say even before I say it... Such knowledge is too wonderful for me, too great for me to know" (See Psalm 139:1–6).

People may not see what you are doing, but there is a God who sees you in your deepest and darkest moments. Always keep your integrity even behind closed doors! Make God proud! Remember that He sees, hears and knows everything!

Living the Lifestyle of Integrity

John Maxwell says "integrity" is "deciding to integrate my heart's value into my daily actions". The single most important quality you can ever develop that will enhance every part of your life is the value of integrity. Living a lifestyle of integrity is the core quality of a successful and happy life. As we read earlier, having integrity means being totally honest and truthful in every part of your life. By making the commitment to become a totally honest person, you will be doing more to ensure your success and happiness in life than anything else you can ever do.

Integrity is a value, like persistence, courage, and intelligence. It is your choice of values and resolution to live by those values that form your character and personality. And it is integrity that enhances all your other values. The quality of person you are is determined by how well you live up to the values that are most important to you. Integrity is the quality that locks in your values and causes you to live consistent with them.

We, as Christians, are called in Matthew 5:8 to be pure in heart, which implies an undivided focus in following God's rule. It calls for no compromise, deviation or avoidance of the price tag that may have to be paid to stand for what we know to be right.

We are also told in Proverbs 11:3: "The integrity of the upright will guide them, but the perversity of the unfaithful will destroy them." According to this verse, integrity guides us to the truth. Integrity is not, in and of itself, the truth. It is a guide for acting on the truth, and it forces you to question and analyze your situation. It is the foundation of character. A person who has a lifestyle of integrity also has an unblemished character in every area of his or her life.

> God knows more about us than we will ever know about ourselves.

One of the most important activities you can engage in is developing your character. And one of the best ways to develop your character is by consistently seeking to please God not man and doing His will.

76

Christ pleases God. Anything the Son does pleases the Father. The Scripture says: "And a voice came from heaven, You are my beloved Son; with you I am well pleased." (See Mark 1:11 ESV)

Living a lifestyle of integrity is acting on biblical principles regardless of your circumstances. God wants us to live a lifestyle of intergrity, because it pleases Him! It is the believer's security in life. It provides you with a sense of wholeness. It gives you an assurance to know when you are walking with the Lord your steps are ordered. This does not mean that bad things will not happen. I assure you they will, remember Joseph's Journey we will all take. But if you are quietly still you will be able to recognize the author of its origin. You will be able to soar above your situation and rest in the arms of an all powerful and mighty God.

Stand Firm And Be Blessed!

In spite of everything that happened to Joseph, he maintained a grateful heart and trusted God absolutely, even in the painful circumstances he was forced to endure. Joseph refused to sin. He was determined to see God glorified in his life. He remained obedient. He continued to be who he was supposed to be — a picture of Christ Jesus.

Beloved, the fact that God has a plan for your life means something incredibly wonderful. It means that the plan was so special that Jesus died on the cross at Calvary to purchase the privilege for you to participate in that plan. You must learn to cling to the determination to participate in that plan. If it is so wonderful that Jesus died on the cross to bring it to fruition, then it is worth your every effort to see it through!

Imagine Joseph's situation. It is obvious that most people in his shoes would be discouraged, angry, fearful, vengeful, and filled with self-pity. We could even understand that he might question God's goodness because the Lord allowed such terrible things to happen to a righteous person. Yet we do not read anything in the Scriptures which indicates that Joseph's attitude was poisoned with any of these "understandable" feelings. Instead, it is clear that the Lord was able to bless and prosper Joseph in all that he did because his heart attitude was right.

> The Lord has not changed. He is still the One who will do everything He has promised you.

When you are a child of destiny, you hav to understand that there is always purpose to your pain. God allows various kinds of suffering to come your way in order to develop the qualities that are necessary for you: humility, obedience and an unselfish attitude. That is why James advice us; "My Christian brothers, you should be happy when you have all kinds of tests. You know these prove your faith. It helps you not to give up. Learn well how to wait so you will be strong and complete and in need of nothing." (James 1:2-4 NLV).

God wants you to be overcomer, strong and mature in your faith; a person who can face a challenge and stand firm. He wants to develop in you the servant attitude which we see so clearly and beautifully portrayed in the life of our Lord Jesus, who learned obedience by the things which He suffered. "Although Jesus was the Son [of God], he learned to be obedient through his sufferings." (Hebrews 5:8 GWT).

The Lord has not changed. He is still the One who will do everything He has promised you. He is in control, Just as the Lord fulfilled His promise to make Joseph a leader over Egypte, He will fulfill His promises to us as believers in Jesus name!

Remain Faithful

In all that happened to Joseph, he remained a man of faithfulness and integrity. You have to understand this, integrity and faithfulness go hand in hand. Integrity is heart honesty. Faithfulness is sticking to your word, no matter what may come your way. Joseph could have easily used his bad times to justify turning away from God and toward sin. But he didn't. He continued to fear God and to turn away from what was evil in His sight. Joseph did what was right. Though his heart had to be breaking from his grief, he maintained his integrity with God and with those around him.

To rise above adversity you must, like Joseph, make the choice to flee sin. You must cultivate the strength of character that causes you to maintain your personal integrity when the pressure is on. You must have faith in God even if you can't see, feel or hear Him.

To have faith in God is to remain faithful to Him, especially during the bad times in life. It is easy to remain faithful to God when things are going well in life but the real test of our faithfulness and integrity to Him is during our trials and sufferings. Sometimes faithfulness to God and His Word sets us on a course where circumstances get worse, not better. It is then that knowing God's promises and His ways are crucial. Joseph remains faithful to the Almighty God through what was probably the worst trial he ever had in his life.

Today, I want you to note; When you become available and open to the move of God in your life, you don't and won't know what is down the road until you get there; you don't and won't know what is around the corner until you turn the corner. Faith in God's future grace for us is what sustains us in those desperate moments.

Joseph Maintained His Integrity

The life of Joseph brings us some powerful lessons of remaining faithful. Rising above adversity, cultivate service, integrity and the ability to put the past behind you and you will find yourself coming out on top in even the most trying of situations.

Brothers and sisters, everyday on the journey to your divine destination, whatever comes, whatever happens, affirm and claim God as the strength and the source of your life. Like Joseph, maintain your intergrity and experience God's faithfulness.

❖ ❖ ❖

"The integrity of the upright will guide them,
but the perversity of the unfaithful
will destroy them."

Proverbs 11:3

Soul Nuggets

1. God knows the answers to all of life's questions.
2. God desires that we be whole or complete in Christ. So that our beliefs, attitudes, words, and actions consistent with His nature.
3. How you live reveals the core of who you are.
4. Everyday on the journey to your divine destination, *whatever comes, whatever happens,* affirm and claim God as the strength and the source of your life.
5. To have faith in God is to remain faithful to Him.

5

JOSEPH
TRAINING CAMP (PRISON)

"Trusting God When Your Dreams Are Shattered"

"Joseph's master took him and put him in prison, the place where the king's prisoners were confined. But while Joseph was there in the prison, the Lord was with him; he showed him kindness and granted him favor in the eyes of the prison warden. So the warden put Joseph in charge of all those held in the prison, and he was made responsible for all that was done there."

Genesis 39:20-22

ONE OF THE STRIKING THINGS about the Law of the Lord is the fact that God authorized no prisons among His people. When a person committed a crime in Israel, their punishment was to be swift and sure, and it was to be a punishment that fit their crime. Yet, throughout history, kings and other rulers have built prisons to contain political enemies and law breakers.

This is still true in our day.

Even though God did not order His people to build any prisons, He did allow some of His most choice servants to spend time in the dungeons of their day. In fact, a few of God's men met their deaths in prison cells. When God allowed one of His servants to go into prison, it wasn't because they were criminals. God sent each of those special prisoners to their prison because He wanted to teach them some lessons they could learn nowhere else. I believe that it is worth our time to consider these prison experiences, because they have much to teach us about our God. With that in mind, let's look at Joseph and his prison experience that I named "Joseph training camp."

As we read in the early chapter, one day when all of the other men were out of the house, Mrs. Potiphar grabbed Joseph's coat and demanded that he sleep with her. Joseph refused and ran from the house, leaving his coat in her hand. To hide her shame and humiliation, Mrs. Potiphar screamed out to the others, with Joseph's coat in her hand as evidence, and accused Joseph of attacking her. Mrs. Potiphar then laid the coat on the bed beside her and awaited her husband's return. She told Mr. Potiphar the same story. Naturally, he became angry and cast Joseph into prison for the alleged attack on his wife.

One may wonder if Potiphar wholly believed the accusation against Joseph since he imprisoned his slave instead of executing him for such a crime. But, in reality, Joseph was there because God wanted to promote him. God used a time of confinement as a time of refinement in the life of Joseph. God prepared him for leadership by sending him to the lockup. In our Christian life, God often do the same thing through His mighty plan to promote us to a greater level of service, but that path will often lead through some prison experience or the other.

Most of the time God's path for us lead us through a time when we are shut off; shut down; shut away and shut up. I have never been in prison, but I understand that prison is not a pleasant place to spend your time. It is a place of problems. Joseph's prison is no different. In Joseph's prison we see mirrored the problems we can expect when God sends us into a prison experience in our own lives. Let's take a look!

Prison here represents time of adversity, bad situation or circumstance.

THE PROBLEMS OF THIS PRISON

—**A Painful Prison**: In Genesis 39:20, we are told that Joseph was "put" into prison. There is no mention of torture of abusive treatment. However, Genesis 40:3 tells us that Joseph was "bound" in this prison. Psalm 105:18, adds even more detail. When all this is considered, it becomes clear that this was a painful time in Joseph's life.

87

Note: It is never easy when the Lord sends you into a prison experience in your life. Of course, God never promised His children that serving Him would be a painless affair. Some of God's most choice servants have been shaped on the harsh anvil of pain; Job (Job 1-2); Paul (2 Corinthians 12:7-10); Elijah (1 Kings 17-19). Even David, a man after God's own heart, was hated and hounded by Saul without reason (1 Samuel 18).

It has been said that; "Those God would use greatly, He firsts hurts deeply." So, you should not be surprised when you find yourself locked away in one of the prisons of life. You are not the first

> Expect to hear God's voice.

one to inhabit the cell of affliction and you will not be the last. But remember, the same God that spoke to Paul in the midst of his storm will speak to you in the midst of your struggle. The same God that revived David in his day of adversity is reaching out to touch your heart with the anointing of the Holy Spirit. Expect to hear God's voice. Open your heart to the Spirit's touch. He is a very present help in the time of adversity.

—A Perplexing Prison: Nowhere are we ever told that Joseph questioned anything that happened to him during his young life. But, surely there had to be questions in his mind. He must have wondered why his brothers hated him so. He must have wondered why he should end up as a slave in Egypt. He must have wondered why he was being punished for doing the right thing. Surely those questions and others must have perplexed his mind.

Note: One of the problems of this prison is that it can be so perplexing in nature. I mean, you try to do your best and live your life for the Lord and still trouble comes your way. That is a troubling truth for many people. And, some are blown off course by the trials they are forced to endure. They throw up their hands and say, "What's the use?" Friend, that is the wrong attitude to take with the trials of life! You may not understand all that is happening, but you can be sure that Lord is in control of the situation.

To complete God's will for your life, you must stop speaking what the enemy is telling you and boldly declare what the Lord is saying. You have to stop complaining about what you see, and start declaring what you want to see. You are the redeemed of the Lord, and God will deliver you out of every adversity life throws at you.

There were some parents who lost their little boy in a tragic automobile accident. They both were very bitter at God. When the pastor came by to see them, the mother said, "Where was God when my son died?" The pastor said, "The same place he was when His Son died." When you take that attitude, you are mistaken. You see, even though the prisons of life are disturbing and distracting, they are part of a plan that you know nothing about.

God is using the hard, harsh events of your life to shape you and move you to where He wants you. You must trust the Lord, even when you can't figure out what He is doing. You need to remember that He has a plan. It is a good plan; it is the best plan, Romans 8:28 says, "And we know that in all things God works for the good of those who love him, who have been called according to his purpose." Our duty is to serve the Lord even when we don't understand Him.

"For my thoughts are not your thoughts, neither are your ways my ways," declares the Lord. "As the heavens are higher than the earth, so are my ways higher than your ways and my thoughts than your thoughts."

Isaiah 55:8-9

No one wants a God they could figure out. Regardless of what life bring your way, you must submit to His will and trust Him to do right. That is what Joseph did. That is what Paul did, and this is what you are to do too.

— **A Prolonged Prison:** We do not know how long Joseph spent in his prison. It was at least two years, but it may have been as long as 13 years, (See Genesis 41). We do know for sure that from the time Joseph was thrown into that pit by his brothers until the day he became the second ruler in Egypt, some 13 years passed by. For and extended period of this man's life, his motto could have been "Nice guys finish last."

Note: Sometimes our trials are over in a short time; at other times they may last for years. God may spend many years shaping your life for a relatively short period of service. He may send you into a prison experience in your life to prepare you for greater service. It took at least 15 years from the time David was anointed king over Israel until he ruled over the land, (See 1 Samuel 16; 2 Samuel 5:4). Those 15 years were hard years; but they were years of development. David was forced to walk through some hard places, but God used that time in his life to develop David to sit on the throne of the land.

Beloved, regardless of how long or how short your prison experiences may be, your duty is to submit to God and to His will for your life.

THE PROVISIONS OF THIS PRISON

This prison is a place of problems, but it also a place filled with God's provisions. He may send us into a prison experience, but He never sends us there alone, or without the resources we will need to survive and thrive in that prison.

—The Provision Of God's Presence: We are told in Genesis 39:21 that "the Lord was with Joseph." That young man went into a prison experience, but he did not go into it or through it alone! The God Who sent him there went with him into that awful place.

Note: Regardless of the nature of the prison experiences you may face in life, remember that God will go with you through them all, Isaiah 43:2 says, "When you go through deep waters, I will be with you. When you go through rivers of difficulty, you will not drown. When you walk through the fire of oppression, you will not be burned up; the flames will not consume you." (NLT). When it came time for Noah to enter the ark, God did not say, "Go into the ark" — He said, "Come into the ark" (See Genesis 7:1). When Shadrach, Meshach and Abednego were thrown into the fiery furnace, they found the Lord was already there (See Daniel. 3:24-25). I want to encourage you with this all time classic hymn by Louisa M. R. Stead.

> "Tis so sweet to trust in Jesus
> Just to take Him at His Word
> Just to rest upon His promise
> And to know, "Thus saith the Lord!"
> Jesus, Jesus, how I trust You
> How I prove You more and more
> Jesus, Jesus, my precious Jesus
> Oh, for grace to trust Him more"

— The Provision Of God's Peace: We are told that God "showed him mercy", (See Genesis 39:20). This word is translated "loving-kindness" in other places in the Old Testament. It carries the same idea as the New Testament word "Grace". In other words, God gave Joseph the power and strength he needed to endure the prison he was forced to face.

Note: He will do the same for you! He says, "My grace is sufficient for you, for my power is made perfect in weakness." (See 2 Corinthians 12:9). Friend, I stand upon this word that there will be grace, peace and power sufficient for the trials you are called upon to face in life in Jesus name!

—The Provision Of God's Promotion: Genesis 39:21 and Genesis 41:14 tell us that even in prison, God was busy using Joseph for His glory. In that horrible dungeon; locked away with the vilest criminals in Egypt; Joseph shone like the star that he was. Why, because Joseph submitted to God's will in the prison experience of his life; God elevated him and used him for His glory.

Note: God does not send us into the prison to bury us there. No! He sends us to prepare us for even greater things in His work. When He allows you to suffer a time of being shut up; shut off and shut it; He does it to grow you so that His image can be more clearly seen in your life. How gold is refined — This is what God is doing in your life through your prison experiences.

In 1 Peter 1:6-8 the Scripture says:

"So be truly glad. There is wonderful joy ahead, even though you have to endure many trials for a little while. These trials will show that our faith is genuine. It is being tested as fire tests and purifies gold – though your faith is far more precious than mere gold. So when your faith remains strong through many trials, it will bring

GOD IS UP TO SOMETHING GREAT

you much praise and glory and honor on the day when Jesus Christ is revealed to the whole world."

John Rippon song "How firm a foundation" describes my point very well; "When through fiery trials thy pathways shall lie, My grace, all sufficient, shall be thy supply; The flame shall not hurt thee; I only design thy dross to consume, and thy gold to refine."

Friend, God sends you into His furnace so that He might use you more greatly for His glory!

THE PRIVILEGES OF THIS PRISON

The problem makes the prison difficult. The provisions make them bearable. But, it is the privileges we find in the prisons of life that cause them to become places of growth and blessing.

—The Privilege Of God's Plan: What kept Joseph going through the dark days of betrayal; deceit and suffering? It was the sure knowledge that God was working out a wonderful plan on Joseph's behalf.

Many years before God had told Joseph that he was going to come out on top. During the broken hearted days when he was betrayed and sold in to slavery by his brothers; Joseph was looking for that plan to be fulfilled. During the hard days when he labored for

Potiphar and fought off the advances of Potiphar's wife; Joseph was waiting for God to do what He said He would do. Then, during the years he languished in that dark, dreary prison; Joseph kept on believing and kept on waiting. He knew his God had made him a promise and that God would keep that promise.

Than the day came! They called him out of prison and brought him before Pharaoh, Joseph interpreted Pharaoh's dream, and was made the second ruler in the kingdom. Yes! This is how God works: mysterious and amazing ways! Only Him can do this! With God all things are possible; there is nothing too small or big that He cannot do! The God we serve is bigger than anything... Joseph had suffered greatly while God worked out His plan; but he remained faithful and he saw God's plan fulfilled in his life. (Genesis. 41:14-36).

Note: You may not understand this, but when God puts you through a prison experience in your life, He has honored you. It is an honor to be counted part of God's plan. To know that "I, as insignificant and as meaningless as I am, am a part of God's plans is an amazing truth". To think that He would take the time to develop you so that He might use you for His glory is a truth too wonderful for words. But, that is one of the things that makes His grace so amazing.

> The God we serve is bigger than anything!

God does not just save you to keep you out of hell. He saves you because you are a part of His eternal plan. He intends to use you for His glory!

"For we are God's handiwork, created in Christ Jesus to do good works, which God prepared in advance for us to do."

Ephesians 2:10

The fact that you are still here and saved today shows that you are important to God. He loves you and He has a plan for your life. So, when your path becomes difficult, believe that He is working out that plan in you and through you.

—The Privilege Of God's Praise: Joseph is careful to give all the glory to the Lord. He knows that God has been working in his life so that God could get glory to His name. God did the things He did in Joseph's life so that He might develop him and use him to show others HIS greatness and glory. We have a mighty GOD! Pharaoh and his nation were introduced to the God of Israel, all because Joseph was submissive to the Lord.

Note: That is what the Lord is doing in our lives when He sends us into a prison experience. He is growing us, but He is also using us to bring more glory to His name. Since that is true, and since our heart's desire ought to be for His glory, there is no greater thing that we can do in life than to submit to His will for our lives, even when we don't understand what the Lord is doing.

Let us pray; *"Father, we embrace Your plans and lay down our own. Have Your way in our lives and let your will be done in our present and future in Jesus name"* Amen!

—The Privilege Of God's Providence: In the end, Joseph saw every promise of the Lord fulfilled and he came to understand that all the pain he was forced to endure served to glorify God; grow him and that it all worked for good in his life, and in the lives of others.

He said to his brothers;

> *"You intended to harm me, but God intended it for good to accomplish what is now being done, the saving of many lives."*

Genesis 50:20

Because of Joseph's obedience and submission, God was able to save the nation of Egypt and the family of Joseph. His brothers had sold him into slavery to get rid of him —But God had orchestrated everything to save the bloodline of the Messiah. (See Genesis 45:5; Psalm 105:17).

Note: In your life, God is going to send you into some places when faith is going to have to swim where reason cannot even wade. During those times, you are going to have to trust God. —You see, when all Joseph

97

could see was the pit, Potiphar's house and the prison; God could see the palace! Our Father in Heaven knows what He is doing in our lives. He knows where He is taking you and I. He knows all about the plans He has for us. He knows what He is preparing us for in this season of our lives. Since we do not know what He is up to! Sometimes all we can see is the prison; during those times, we must trust that He sees the palace.

> In your life, God is going to send you into some places when faith is going to have to swim where reason cannot even wade.

Also we must submit ourselves to God's authority and obey His Word. Submission and obedience isn't about intention, it is all about action. Your obedience releases your blessings. So friend, no matter what comes your way, do the right things and keep on serving the Lord. Always remember, those who won't serve God in the prisons of life are not fit to serve Him the palaces of life either.

Maybe you are in some kind of a prison experience in your life? ... What are you doing in that prison? Are you rebelling against it, or submitting to it? Just like Joseph, God has you there for one reason: He is using that prison as a tool of preparation for a future promotion.

Let me give you two great "Prison Promises" verses from the Living Word. And I pray that these

98

verses will sustain you when all you can see is the prison.

—**Romans 8:28;** "And we know that all things work together for good to them that love God, to them who are the called according to his purpose."

—**Psalm 138:8;** "The Lord will vindicate me; your love, Lord, endures forever— do not abandon the works of your hands."

Friend, God's favor can reach you in your prison experience, just like Joseph, and finally promote you to the palace. Today, refuse to be fearful about what will happen to you. Be patient in your prison experience because... God is leading you to meet your butler. In fact, He is about to fix some things in your life and put some things in alignment!

❖ ❖ ❖

"Trust in the LORD with all your heart, and do not lean on your own understanding. In all your ways acknowledge him, and he will make straight your paths"

Proverbs 3:5-6

Soul Nuggets

1. God is using the hard, harsh events of your life to shape you and move you to where He wants you. You must trust the Lord, even when you can't figure out what He is doing.
2. God does not send us into prison experiences to bury us there. He sends us to prepare us for even greater things in His work.
3. The same God that spoke to Paul in the midst of his storm will speak to you in the midst of your struggle. The same God that revived David in his day of adversity is reaching out to touch your heart with the anointing of the Holy Spirit.
4. Your obedience releases your blessings.
5. Those who won't serve God in the prisons of life are not fit to serve Him the palaces of life either.
6. God has you there for one reason: He is using that prison as a tool of preparation for a future promotion.

6

JOSEPH USED

HIS GIFT

"Bloom Where You are Planted"

"Each one should use whatever gift he has received to serve others, faithfully administering God's grace in its various forms."

1 Peter 4:10

LIFE CAN SOMETIMES BE TOUGH, and you can feel as though you are the dirt that the rooftop gardener is ripping apart; however, in that soil that is been crumbled and torn into tiny pieces is where a new flower is planted to grow and blossom. Life may not be ideal where you are, but it is in that broken and aerated soil that God wishes to grow a beautiful flower; YOU! The Master Gardener wants you to bloom where you are planted!

As we Christians walk through life's pathway, striving to reach the goal God has set before us, we need to always remember that our Father in heaven has given each of us abilities and desires that coincide with His plans for us; we need to use those gifts and talents for His glory. But what happens when our desires do not fit with the gifts and talents that He has given us? It has been said, "He who buries his talent is making a grave mistake." How true this statement is for so many of us.

Have you ever stopped to ponder the truth that God created you with your specific abilities and talents for a reason? No one else on this earth is like you. There never has been anyone and there never will be anyone like you. You are special and unique! You were created on purpose, with purpose, for purpose. You are here for a reason.

Hear what the Lord says:

> *"Before I formed you in the womb I knew you,*
> *before you were born I set you apart;..."*
> **Jeremiah 1:5a**

Through the Holy Spirit God has empowered each believer (You and I) with a unique abilities, talents, and spiritual gifts that He wills us to use for His glory and to benefit others, but we often times don't use them, especially in times of adversity.

The Bible says in 1 Corinthians 12:4-6: "There are different kinds of gifts, but the same Spirit distributes them. There are different kinds of service, but the same Lord. There are different kinds of working, but in all of them and in everyone it is the same God at work."

104

God's gifts and powers are available to all of us. It is our right and responsibility to accept our spiritual gifts, multiply our talents, and share them. As Peter said, God has given each of us a gift from His great variety of spiritual gifts. That we should use them well to serve one another. (See 1 Peter 4:10).

Now tell me, what are the gifts that God has given you? How are you using them to serve God and your generation? I know our Heavenly Father has given you specific gifts to be used for His purposes. How do I know? Because I believe that there are many gifts, and to every man is given a gift by the Spirit of God.

To whom much is given, much is required — not expected, but required. God places high regard on stewardship, and He expects His people to become faithful stewards as well. Paul wrote; "So let a man think of us as Christ's servants, and stewards of God's mysteries. Here, moreover, it is required of stewards, that they be found faithful." (See 1 Corinthians 4:1, 2 WEB). God inspired Paul to make it clear that He requires His people to be faithful stewards of all that He gives them.

A steward is someone who has been entrusted with the possessions or affairs of someone else with the understanding that he is to care for them and manage them responsibly. God is looking for an increase from us. By doing our very best by growing in stewardship and not floating or doing nothing, we fulfill what Christ says in Luke 16:10, "Whoever can be trusted with very little can also be trusted with much, and whoever is dishonest with very little will also be dishonest with much."

The story of Joseph teaches us to stay faithful stewards in adversity. In the midst of his Egyptian test, after his pride had been cut down to size, he remained faithful to whatever God gave him to do. He became a faithful slave in Potiphar's house. Even when he was tempted and coerced, he remained faithful. He was then falsely accused and thrown into prison: even there he stayed faithful. He became so excellent in character that the warden handed all of the responsibilities of the jail over to him.

The Bible says:

"The Lord was with Joseph and extended kindness to him, and gave him favor in the sight of the chief jailer."

Genesis 39:21

Now the question is why did Joseph excel even in the midst of this adversity? Was it his dream to become the prison warden? Did he say, "My destiny is to be the warden of this jail, so I'm going to manipulate things to work my way up"? That sentence isn't in my Bible. God prospered Joseph because of his faithfulness while he was "out of season." He was not in the prime season of his life; he was in the preparatory season. His ultimate dream, his destiny

The Master Gardener wants you to bloom where you are planted!

was yet to be realized.

Brothers and sisters, to fulfill our purpose, we must realize that it is often in the desert of anonymity and obscurity that God molds and shapes our characters, making us ready on the inside for all He has for us. Unfortunately it is also during these times of waiting and preparation that we are most vulnerable to growing weary and giving up on having and doing God's "all."

> To whom much is given, much is required—not expected, but required.

The enemy tries to convince us that our dreams for extraordinary living are not worth the wait, too difficult, or even impossible to achieve. But the devil is a liar! God has put a dream of greatness in your heart and He wants you to fulfill it.

You see, if anybody had a right to have a bad attitude and feel sorry for himself, Joseph did. But Joseph realized that God had placed leadership qualities and administrative skills in him, so he continued to develop his potential in spite of his negative circumstances. He was falsely accused and thrown into prison, but he kept using the gifts God had given him, even there. Joseph did the right things although wrong things were happening to him. Because of his persistence and his discipline, he continued to rise to the top, eventually becoming the second highest official in the country of Egypt.

Joseph learned everything he needed to learn at the anvil of adversity in order to become the second most powerful man on the earth. He didn't enroll in a Pharaoh School nor did he attend Egypt Tech. Instead, he went to "Adversity-University" where he remained faithful by using his God-given gifts and talents, in spite of everything. He didn't cast off the adversity, and say, "I'm a failure. Adversity hit me: I'm never going to be used by God." No! Joseph did the best out of what was given to him. Even the smallest things he was truthful and the Lord was with him and blessed everything that he did.

In the same way, in our lives the Lord wants us to do our very best in every situation. Don't wait for the day when you will get the best and then do the things from that. Whatever talents or resources you have got, do the best and the Lord will bless you abundantly. Never be in a attitude that "someday when God gives me the things I will do it but be in a attitude that I will to the best with what I have today and not for tomorrow!"

> God is looking for an increase from us.

The Lord wants you to bloom where you are planted; so don't wait for everything to be ideal before you give your best. He wants you to live life beyond limitations! He has ordained for your life to be full of His glory through Christ Jesus. There is no limit to how glorious and

108

blissful your life should be. There is no end to your prosperity, victory, success, and advancement! No matter where you live or what life circumstances you find yourself in, you can make the choice to succeed, regardless of your challenges. Don't ever give up! Keep going! From today, use the gifts, talents, intellect and abilities you have, and stop complaining about what you lack! Step up to a higher level and make the best of what you have!

Living Beyond the Limits!

Stop and think for a moment. Why do people live below God's grace upon their lives? How can the talented and anointed be frustrated? What would our lives look like if we didn't put limitations on what God could do? Many of us cannot get to the place where God wants us to be due to the "Limitations" that we have placed on Him. We limit God's ability to protect, provide and prevail for us. The Psalmist says: "Great is our Lord and mighty in power; his understanding has no limit." (Psalm 147:5).

Dear friend, the God that we worship is the God who has no limits. He is the God who is not limited by space, knowledge, and power. With Him there is no limit to what you can do. There is no obstacle you can't overcome. Through Him, all things are possible. The Apostle Paul knew the power of God was working in him when he said: "I can do all this through him who gives me strength." (See Philippians 4:13). He was persuaded that Christ was his strength and he could do all things. This statement applies to you. You can rephrase it and say, "I can do all things through Christ who strengthens me." In other words, Jesus lives in you, and He strengthens you. In Him, you can do all things!

"All things" means there is no limit to what you can do. There is no limit to what God can do in you and through you! God has given you everything you need to be successful in accomplishing His purposes in your life. He created you, equipped you, and then filled you with His Holy Spirit, to face situations and that, with His help and guidance you will enter into your divine destination.

> God has put a dream of greatness in your heart and He wants you to fulfill it.

As we go through life, we at times encounter places where our faith is stretched beyond its limits. These are the crossroads and crisis times where our trust in God's ability to deliver us seems to be less than sufficient. As I highlighted previously, one of the great problems of our day is that people excuse themselves from doing their best or getting involved because the circumstances are not ideal! But God wants us to be diligent, use our gifts and talents, and do our best even if the circumstances are not ideal. He wants us to be a

110

faithful steward of the gifts and abilities He has given us.

Beloved, God wants you to believe that with Him all things are possible. Even though you may be weak, through Jesus Christ there is no limit to what you can do.

No matter where you are in life right now, God has much more in store for you. He wants to take you to new levels in every area of your life. He wants to give you more wisdom so you can make better decisions. He wants to give you stronger anointing so you can have greater influence. God wants to bless you financially so you can be a blessing to those in need.

Don't get stuck in the same old rut! There is so much more to life! God has new frontiers for you to explore and higher mountains for you to climb! God wants you to understand He will strengthen you. You have no excuse not to be victorious. Jesus has made it all possible for you. That is hard for you to even imagine, because most of your frustrations in life are a direct result of limitations. But understand this, you are a super-victor in Christ Jesus! His Victory is your victory! His Life is your life! His Peace and His Joy are yours too!

God has freely given you everything in Christ you need to be victorious. Therefore, there are no limits in fulfilling God's purpose and plan for your life. I can tell you with great confidence that your best days are right out in front of you! Loose yourself from limitation and boundary. Tap into your gifts and talents. That is where your success is!

Like Bishop Jakes said, "Get ready! Get ready! Get ready...!

Destiny Is Waiting For You

In Jeremiah 1:5, God said; "Before I formed you in the womb I knew you, before you were born I set you apart; I appointed you as a prophet to the nations." Wow! Isn't that awesome? God knew your name before time began... Before the foundation of the world He approves you unconditionally. The psalmist wrote that the days of his life were "fashioned" for him. You too were born at a particular time and to a particular family in a particular location.

God made your life a set number of years in a set environment so you could be and do all that He created you to be and do. If you have ever wondered why you are on this earth, understand that God has placed you here as a unique person with a unique mission aimed at establishing and extending His kingdom on earth as it is in heaven. Your potential lies securely and completely in that purpose.

God wants you to be involved with His work. He has a unique role for you to play in His plan for this generation. This is your ministry, and God has gifted you for this assignment: to perform a function within

112

the body of Christ with supernatural joy, energy, and effectiveness. He wants you to know Him more so He can reveal His glory through you. The Father wants to promote you to new levels of victory, so you can live that abundant life that He has promised you! He desires to do exceedingly, abundantly above and beyond what you could ask, think or imagine. (See Ephesians 3:20).

Today, begin to think the way God thinks. Think increase! Think Big! Think expansion! For the path of the righteous grows brighter, and brighter, and brighter. Start expecting the unexpected and look at life through your eyes of faith. When you do, God will show up and begin to work things out in your favor.

> Don't get stuck in the same old rut! There is so much more to life!

You are packaged by God to be the best. God has giving you talents and abilities so that you can enjoy the fullness of life. When you live below the divine investments in your life, there is a problem. Why? We serve a God of increase! He wants us to continually rise up higher in Him. When God created us, He made an investment in us, and He expects a return on that investment.

The waiting is over and it is your season to step into what God has prepared for you by using your gifts and talents. You cannot wait for your dreams to be fulfilled and then start developing your amazing

113

gifts. Waiting on the fulfillments is too late. You have to start developing now by using them! Can you imagine the disaster Joseph would have been in if he came to his place of fulfillment undeveloped and immature, with unpolished skills? Joseph embraced and cultivated his gift, he could boldly respond to both the royal officers and to Pharaoh "Please tell them to me" (See Genesis 40:8 ESV).

Using and developing your spiritual gifts will allow you to confidently respond in situations that call for them.

Also Joseph does not allow pride to enter in, but always gives God the credit: "Do not interpretations belong to God?" (See Genesis 40:8), "It is not in me; God will give Pharaoh a favorable answer" (See Genesis 41:16). Joseph understood that pride takes a good thing from the Creator God and attributes it to the created being. As he uses his gifts, Joseph humbly reminds those involved that it is God's work, not Joseph's work. Your spiritual gifts must result in glory being given to God. When you live for the glory of God, you are doing what you were created to do. And you become who you were created to be.

This is what God says in Isaiah 43:6-7; "Bring my sons from afar and my daughters from the end of the earth, everyone who is called by my name, whom I created for my glory, whom I formed and made." Whoever you are, wherever you have come from, your reason for existence on planet earth is the same. You have been created for the glory of God to take all that you are and all that you have and use it to magnify God. For every good gift and every perfect gift is from above, and comes down from the Father of lights, with whom there is no variation or shadow of turning. (See James 1:17).

> When you live for the glory of God, you are doing what you were created to do.

What are you afraid off? In Exodus 33, God's promises His presence in the time of your trial. He said; "My presence will go with you, and I will give you rest." God has a purpose for every trial that comes into your life. Nothing happens to you without God's approval or purpose. He has the power to work things out to your good. He created you, equipped you, and then filled you with His Holy Spirit, to face any situation.

Regardless of the circumstances you are facing God can make all things work to your good and to your benefit. He loves to do above and beyond and show Himself strong on your behalf. God's perspective is not the same as yours. He sees the purpose and outcome of your trial. All you and I see is the pain and the problem. God sees the future while all we see is the present. Nothing misses the Father's eye. He can see your faithfulness during your own process of fulfilling the dream He has placed in your heart: your own preparatory season of life.

I encourage you to develop, and bring to full maturity everything that God has given you, even in the time of testing. This is the right moment to release that gift, that talent to glorify God and to benefit others! You have treasure in you. You have skill and talent. Start sharpening them! When God sees that you are prepared, then He will open new doors of opportunity.

I pray that God removes any bondage and blindness and allow you to see opportunities for advancing His Kingdom in Jesus name! Your best days are ahead of you. GO!

The Creation Is Eagerly Awaiting

In Romans 8:19 the Bible says, "...the creation is eagerly awaiting the revelation of God's children," In other words all creation is waiting, yearning for the time you and I (God's children) will come upon the world stage!

You see, this world has one major need right now in the 21st Century. The world doesn't need another politician telling the people what they want to hear. The world doesn't need a steady robust economy to help it through the hard times that have been prophesied upon it. No! The world needs the sons of God to arrive on the scene. Why? Because we have something that all mortals walking the face of the earth must have. We have the Key that will set the whole creation free. And that Key is JESUS, the Light of the world!

Jesus said: "I am the light of the world. Whoever follows me will never walk in darkness, but will have the light of life." (See John 8:12).

John also confirmed this in John 12:36a; "Believe in the light while you have the light, so that you may become children of light."

Today believe that you are the Most High God's elect, His child created in His image, and you are what this world needs. "You are the light of the world — like a city on a hilltop that cannot be hidden." (See Matthew 5:14 NLT).

You are part of the ones who will have cut through all of the deception and vice in this world system. You are part of those who sees the Spirit and walk in the Spirit and filled with the Spirit of the living GOD. And with your gifts and talents you will build the old waste places and build the spiritual walls to the heavenly city. (See Isaiah 58:12 NLT).

Beloved, once again you need to understand and believe that God created you for a special purpose and has a divine plan for your life.... so don't let your current situation or the devil sidetrack you. Don't say I don't have any talent or a gift. The Scripture make it clear that; "We are God's workmanship, created in Christ Jesus to do good works, which God prepared in advance for us to do." (See Ephesians 2:10). Apostle Peter also wrote; "Each of you should use whatever gift you have received to serve others, as faithful stewards of God's grace in its various forms." (1Peter 4:10)

God makes no mistakes; He makes beauty, love, kindness and goodness. God created you, your heart, your brain and your soul for a purpose. Without your existence this world would be incomplete. You are a gift from God to the world. The time has come to impact your generation. I decree and declare that your life will serve a purpose!

Your job on this earth is to search out that purpose and fulfill it. Search deep within to find those gifts and talents that God bestowed so generously upon you so many years ago. Then use those gifts to their fullest potential. Remember, it is what you do with what you have that makes you who you are.

> God has a purpose for every trial that comes into your life. Nothing happens to you without God's approval or purpose.

I believe that God wants to plant us where we can be faithful witnesses so that others might see us grow and bloom into what Christ wants us to be. So listen for God's call and no matter where you find yourself along life's journey bloom where you are planted, so that Christ might shine in and through you.

118

I pray that from today you will treasure every gift that God has given you, every opportunity that He has made possible for you and every relationship that He has given to you... I pray that you will always have an attitude of gratitude and not murmur and complain about your life, for God gives good gifts to all of His people, at all times.

I pray that you will give freely to others out of your abundance as God blesses you and you will not be selfish with your blessings, especially when you have the opportunity to bless someone in need, in JESUS name! Amen!!!

❖ ❖ ❖

"Now it is required that those who have been given a trust must prove faithful. "

1 Corinthians 4:2

Soul Nuggets

1. Life may not be ideal where you are, but it is in that broken and aerated soil that God wishes to grow a beautiful flower, YOU!
2. God has given each believer unique abilities, talents, and spiritual gifts that He wills us to use for His glory and to benefit others.
3. God wants you to be involved with His work.
4. God has a purpose for every trial that comes into your life.
5. Nothing happens to you *without* God's approval or purpose.
6. You have treasure in you.
7. God sees the future while all you and I see is the present.
8. When God created us, He made an investment in us, and *He expects a return* on that investment.
9. Remember, it is what you do with what you have that makes you who you are.

7

JOSEPH DREAM DELAYED BUT NOT DENIED

"Greater Is Coming!"

"For all the promises of God in Him are Yes, and in Him Amen, to the glory of God through us."

2 Corinthians 1:20

HAVE YOU EVER HAD A GOD inspired dream that didn't happen as quickly as you thought it should? What if you have done your part by "believing," but you haven't seen any results? Is there something you don't understand? Is there something else you need to do to see God's promises fulfilled? If you are searching for answers to these kinds of questions, I encourage you to read this chapter believing that the same God who brought you from *there* (Your Past) to *here* (Your Present) will take you from *here* (Your Present) to *there* (Your Future).

There are periods of our lives in which it is easy to

believe. There are also periods in which questions come. We don't go looking for the doubts, but they come looking for us. We join a long line of people who have been asked to believe something that seems impossible from our perspective. This is especially true when your dream becomes a nightmare and you find yourself in the starring role.

As you looked at the shattered remains of your plans and dreams, asking "Why"? And hear the pastor speak about how God loves you and He has a plan for your life. We believe, we want to believe, but there are times that it seems impossible. This brings many questions; How should we respond when God's promises seem impossible? How do we continue waiting on God especially when we are pregnant with purpose?

Every person must face the difficulty that comes when God's timing does not line up with our own. What is the desperate job seeker to do when the employment doesn't come through? How does the married couple face another childless year when everyone around them has caught the pregnancy bug? How much longer does the single woman have to wait for a good man? Will science ever find a cure for the illness plaguing the young person in chronic pain?

Our response to these sometimes gnawing questions is a matter of faith: Do you really believe that God loves you; that He has given you every spiritual blessing; that even in the midst of heartache He is working for the good; that He is truly

124

trustworthy? —Often when our prayers are not answered and our faith waivers we have a choice to make. We can stay stuck in doubt or we can choose to trust God's timing and believe what the Bible says about His plans for our lives.

God Has a Timing... Wait on Him!

In this hurry-up world, waiting for anything can cause us to lose our tempers, tongues, and good senses more frequently than we care to admit. I don't know anyone who enjoys waiting in line. We don't like waiting at stoplights. We don't like waiting for dinner. We don't even like waiting on God. We want what we want now!

Perhaps we misunderstand what waiting is all about. The free dictionary defines waiting as "The act of remaining inactive or stationary." But for us believes waiting is not passive. It is an activity. It is quiet, active stillness. It is a directed, purposeful expectancy. Waiting on God is a definite directing of our attention toward Him, waiting for His intervention in our circumstances and waiting for further instructions.

We are all waiting on God at different times in our lives. For you, it could be that baby you have been longing to hold in your arms, an illness to be healed, a family member or friend to come to the Lord, a break-

GOD IS UP TO SOMETHING GREAT

> The same God who brought you from your past to your present will take you from your present to your future.

through in your marriage or finances, to start a business, a door to be opened, what ever it is we are left waiting. You have probably heard the old saying "good things come to those who wait."

Sometimes it is hard to understand why God doesn't allow things to happen straightaway. All the while people keep telling you to trust in God and the right thing will come along and to be honest they start to sound like just words. 'Platitudes with not much meaning. They lose their impact and you start to lose a bit of hope; What if God isn't going to answer my prayer? Time is running out. How do I keep trusting when it seems like nothing is changing?

Listen, some things can never be rushed. An excellent example is the birth of a baby. There will always be a waiting period of approximately nine months from the time a child is conceived to when he or she is born. Some things actually turn out better when we wait for them. The skin of a banana has a green color when it is plucked off a tree. But the banana will taste better if you wait until the skin turns yellow before eating it. Other items like cheese taste better when they are "aged."

I am not going to deny that waiting on God is hard. But an important lesson that I am continuing to learn each day is that God works things out in His own perfect timing. Trusting in God, I believe is the key to success and happiness in life.

Many people in the Bible have had to go through times of waiting. Noah and his family didn't sit in the ark for only 40 days while it rained. They waited for over a year until the floodwaters subsided and the birds Noah sent out found dry land. How would you like being confined in the ark that whole time with all those smelly animals? God promised Abraham and Sarah a son from their own loins but had to wait 25 years before Isaac was born. David was anointed King of Israel at the age of 16 but didn't possess the throne until he was 30. At the beginning of Joseph's story, we are told he dreamt of family members bowing down to him. But he waited 13 years until he saw that come to pass.

Brothers and sisters, when God gives you a promise you must understand there will come a testing time to see if you are going to be faithful to Him and deserving of the promise. In Ecclesiastes the Bible declares that, "there is a season for everything." Likewise, in our lives, there are seasons when things go well, ones where it seems like most areas in our lives are lying fallow and there are inevitable seasons of struggles. The trick is to learn to trust God in every season. God uses seasons of struggle to purify us, to show us what we need to work on. Those things that we think are so bad, Paul calls "light afflictions".

"For our light affliction, which is but for a moment, worketh for us a far more exceeding and eternal weight of glory;"

2 Corinthians 4:17

Seasons of struggle don't last always. And with each temporary setback comes opportunities for fresh commitment and renewal. God is rich in mercy. He always has a specific reason for telling us to wait. Our responsibility is to trust Him. Trust that He has a purpose for His delay. When I wanted to release my first album (Victory Noise), I didn't understand why God wanted me to wait and help others to finish their projects while I thought mine is ready to be released. But, a year later, I realized the Lord had saved me from beginning my music ministry internationally without a solid foundation and a good plan.

Some things actually turn out better when we wait for them.

While you wait, God works behind the scenes on your behalf. A lack of trust is perhaps the root cause behind your decisions to jump ahead in disobedience. What arrogance to think we can work things out better than God can. Being impatient can cause you to forfeit God's blessings from coming into your life. Give Him time to arrange every detail so you will receive His best. When you have done everything right but results aren't forthcoming as quickly as you expect, don't give up because your time is surely coming. It took two years before Joseph's efforts in the prison produced a result, but when it did, what a result! Though his former cellmate promptly forgot all about him when he was released and restored to his old position, it was for a reason and Joseph did not lose hope (See Genesis 40).

Let's imagine for a minute that the king's butler did not forget about Joseph and told the king about him immediately. The best thing that could have happened from that scenario would be that Joseph would also be restored to his former position as a slave because the king didn't need him yet! Isn't that interesting? God waited until Joseph was needed at the very highest level in the land before allowing his former cellmate to remember him. By that time, the king was troubled by his own dream, not just worried, but troubled! I love it! He was desperate for a solution and would give anything to get it.

Do you think Joseph could have asked for that level of compensation had he been asked to 'name his price'? Don't you think the reward the king gave for the translation of his dream was very generous to say the least? The wisdom of the due season lies in understanding that due seasons always come. The problem is not when God, the issue is making sure that you are prepared when your appointed time shows up. Don't spend time worrying about whether God's Word will come to pass in your life; instead, spend time preparing for the promise.

The Word must come to pass because it is "Yea" and "Amen"! Meanwhile, if you are not prepared when the Word shows up you will miss the promise. In Galatians 4:1-4, the Bible makes it clear that God will not give any breakthrough to any Christian who is not prepared. From God's perspective, preparation expedites the manifestation. The manifestation is set for an appointed time; but one can miss the divine moment due to lack of preparation.

> God is rich in mercy. He always has a specific reason for telling us to wait.

God told you He would give you the house, the car, the mate, the work, ect. But wait! However, you may often throw a spiritual temper tantrum and begin to question God's timing. If the truth were told, God hasn't released the promise because you are not ready to handle it yet. The power to possess your promise lies in your persistence to prepare. Persistence in preparation prepares you for your promise! Without preparation you cannot possess the promise.

"Be patient, therefore, brothers, until the coming of the Lord. See how the farmer waits for the precious fruit of the earth, being patient about it, until it receives the early and

the late rains. You also, be patient. Establish your hearts, for the coming of the Lord is at hand."

James 5:7-8 (ESV)

Regardless of what you are waiting for, you must fully understand the purpose of God's waiting process. God uses the waiting process to prepare you for the blessings He has in store for you. Maybe you need to work on your attitude, deal with your insecurities, be healed emotionally, or be delivered from fear. Whatever your "issue" is and however long it takes, you must embrace the waiting process and trust God's divine timing. If He gives you the promise now, it would literally overwhelm you. The hard part is not getting the promise, but rather whether you will be able to keep it.

God wants you to have "fruit" that remains. In this season of your life, you have to trust that God knows the appointed time to release His best for you. All you need to do is hold on until your change comes. God has always been trustworthy and faithful and will never leave or forsake you. Like the old folks used to say, "He may not come when you want Him, but He is always on time." God never forgets and even when it looks like nothing is happening, He continues to orchestrate things in the background so that at the right time, the outcome will be super abundantly above what you could have imagined!

The Scripture declares in Ephesians 3, with God's

power working in us, God can do much, much more than anything we can ask or imagine. When God is the actor on the stage of a person's life, all the other actors will disappear. Any force or power hindering what God has promised in your life will wither in the name of Jesus!

Even though the promise seems delayed, it is not denied! God is still working on you and the plans He has for you are good plans. The thoughts He has for you are good thoughts and it is God's perfect will for you to encounter His blessing in your home, in your family and in your life. But in order to extend into the greater blessing of God there must be a circumcision of the mind, the heart, the soul and the spirit by spending time in His presence.

Do you want to intimately experience the Lord's presence and a greater blessing? If so, I challenge you to...;

—**Rejoice in the Lord always:** Philippians 4:4 says; "Rejoice in the Lord always: and again I say, rejoice." When Paul was writing the letter to the Philippians he was in prison, his feet were bound yet he was encouraging others to rejoice. When he and Silas were imprisoned, they sang praises when naturally, they should have been crying. Their praises generated an earthquake which set them free, including other prisoners.

The reason you should rejoice is the fact that you know that your God will deliver *you* from trouble. You know that your redeemer lives.

"Be joyful always; pray continually; give thanks in all circumstances, for this is God's will for you in Christ Jesus."

1 Thessalonians 5:16-18

— Commit your ways unto the Lord and trust Him: That is, bring your burdens to Him; stop bearing the load, take the pressure off your head. Refuse to listen to the problem that is continually making its presence felt. Don't turn your solution into a problem. Solution is to make things easy but many people turn it into problems; they give God conditions for serving Him. No! Instead, rely solely upon the Lord.

Sometimes God says no to that need. As hard as that may be, trust in Him. When He says "NO" consider it protection. He knows everything, even the unseen and the future. You have to trust in the master plan He has for your life, and keep living. — Believe that His Word is truth and have complete confidence in Him.

> The power to possess your promise lies in your persistence to prepare.

Psalm 111:7 says;

"The works of his hands are faithful and just; all his precepts are trustworthy."

—**Do not give up:** Know that God who has promised will surely bring it to pass. Wait patiently upon Him. Don't allow the blessings meant for you go to someone else because the Lord said: "My word that goes out from my mouth: It will not return to Me empty, but will accomplish what I desire and achieve the purpose for which I sent it." (Isaiah 55:11). When you have a promise from God, you can be certain about the outcome. Keep standing in faith with a joyful attitude, a thankful attitude, and hold on to the promise. I believe it will surely come to pass.

—**Persevere:** Remain steadfast, do not drop any thing you are doing for God because there is a problem. Be a source of blessing to others around you. I can assure you, you are not the only one waiting for something. Look around you. You can be the answer to someone else's prayer. By helping others around you, your problems don't seem so big anymore and you actually feel better. You could even seek additional responsibility and refuse to yield to ridicule, discouragement and frustration in your faith and in your trust in God.

> When He says "NO" consider it protection. He knows everything, even the unseen and the future.

Always remember, it is not how fast you go that matters but how well. Whatever you are doing, you must persist in your prayers. For the Bible says: "Blessed is the man who remains steadfast under trial, for when he has

Joseph Dream Delayed But Not Denied

stood the test he will receive the crown of life, which God has promised to those who love him." (James 1:12 ESV).

—Live in the present: Worrying about the future robs you of the present. Worrying would not change your situation so enjoy your life and appreciate God's goodness in your life. Count your blessings, name them one by one. Develop yourself while waiting. Read books, meet people, develop your talent so that you are ready when that job comes, when that husband comes, when that baby comes, when that breakthrough comes. Focus on what you have and not on what you don't have.

"But I the Lord will speak what I will, and it shall be fulfilled without delay. For in your days, you rebellious people, I will fulfill whatever I say, declares the Sovereign Lord."

Ezekiel 12:25

Our God is not inactive or silent while we wait on Him. He said; "I will speak what I will, and it shall be fulfilled without delay!... I will fulfill whatever I say!" God is not a man that He should lie. If He promised it, He will fulfill!

Commit your ways unto the Lord and trust Him. That is, bring your burdens to Him.

During seasons of waiting He continues to work in us. While waiting might seem a waste of time, God

135

designed it to be productive. The exercise of waiting is shaping and sharpening. Through it God instills humility, patience and peace in our hearts and minds. It's been said that we do not know what the future holds, but we believe in a God who holds our future.

Since God is beyond time, He fully abides in the past, present and future. In the same way that we view our surroundings at this precise moment, God just as clearly sees every day in everyone's life throughout all of history. Although we may never understand why and when God chooses to work, we rest in the hands of a God who gave His life for us. Like the Psalmist we can faithfully proclaim to the Lord,

❖ ❖ ❖

"But as for me, I trust in You, O Lord, I say, "You are my God." My times are in Your hand;"

Psalm 31:14-15

God's Inspirational Promises About Patience And Waiting

Isaiah 40:31
"But those who wait on the Lord shall renew their strength; They shall mount up with wings like eagles, They shall run and not be weary, They shall walk and not faint."

Joseph Dream Delayed But Not Denied

John 13:7
*"Jesus replied, "You do not realize now what I am doing,
but later you will understand."*

2 Peter 3:9
*"The Lord is not slow in keeping his promise, as some
understand slowness. Instead he is patient with you, not
wanting anyone to perish, but everyone to come to
repentance."*

Deuteronomy 30:16
*"Be still before the Lord and wait patiently for him; do not
fret when people succeed in their ways, when they carry out
their wicked schemes. Refrain from anger and turn from
wrath; do not fret—it leads only to evil. For those who are
evil will be destroyed, but those who hope in the Lord will
inherit the land."*

Habakkuk 2:3
*"For the revelation awaits an appointed time; it speaks of the
end and will not prove false. Though it linger, wait for it; it
will certainly come and will not delay."*

Psalm 27:14
*"Wait for the Lord; be strong and take heart and wait
for the Lord"*

*You can pre-order a copy of my next book "Standing On God's
Promises" for more GOD'S INSPIRATIONAL PROMISES.*

Soul Nuggets

1. There are periods of our lives in which it is easy to believe. There are also periods in which questions come.
2. For us believes waiting is not passive. It is an activity. It is quiet, active stillness. It is a directed, purposeful expectancy.
3. Whatever your "issue" is and however long it takes, you must embrace the waiting process and trust God's divine timing.
4. There is a season for everything.
5. The same God who brought you from THERE (Your Past) to HERE (Your Present) will take you from HERE (Your Present) to THERE (Your Future).
6. It is God's perfect will for you to encounter His blessing in your home, in your family and in your life.
7. Stay in His presence with a joyful attitude, a thankful attitude, and STAND on His WORD!
8. Develop yourself while waiting.

8

JOSEPH: FROM PRISON TO PALACE

"When God Turns Evil to Good"

"You intended to harm me, but God intended it for good to accomplish what is now being done, the saving of many lives."

Genesis 50:20

LIFE IS A SERIES OF PROBLEM and God has a purpose behind every problem that we encounter. Any trial a believer faces can ultimately bring glory to God because God can bring good out of any bad situation. When trouble comes, do you grumble, complain, and blame God, or do you see your problems as opportunities to honor Him? God is in the business of changing and turning people's life around by giving them not only second chance, but a fresh start.

He says, "See, I am doing a new thing! Now it springs up; do you not perceive it? I am making a way in the wilderness and streams in the wasteland." (See

Isaiah 43:19).

Our God is a Creative God, always doing something new. His laws and principles never change but His blessings are new every morning. His thoughts are not as our thoughts —neither are His ways as our ways. The One who called the end before the beginning said He is doing a new thing in your life! Just because you don't see it doesn't mean it hasn't started. The Bible declares; "It is going to spring forth". In other words, it isn't something in the future! If God were to show you right now the good that He has in store for your life, I believe it would boggle your mind.

We have trained our brains to 'think' that if something seems to be 'going wrong' (not according to our plan or not how God told us the end would be), then we must be doing something wrong. But that is one of the many ways that 'religion' or 'tradition' has been able to lie to us and it can get us to live lives of compromise, complacency, mediocrity, and conformity. This is a place where we never really get out of the box and we never let God out of the box either.

> God has a purpose behind every problem that we encounter.

Why do you try to put God into a box? God created all the boxes in the universe! He is only going to fit into one if He chooses to do so, and even then, that

142

would be some BOX! Yet you are constantly trying to squeeze God into a shape of your choosing. Friend, never underestimate and limit God! If God said He will take you from the prison to the palace then believe it shall come to pass! If God said it, He will do it! If God spoke it, He will bring it to pass!

Regardless of your circumstances, you don't have to spend one more day of your life worried, uncertain or stressed out. You may have seen God's goodness in the past, but it is nothing compared to what He has prepared for your future. God is shifting things in your direction. New and unprecedented favor is coming your way. He has called you, equipped you, empowered you and chosen you for great things. Get ready to receive what He has already set in motion for your life.

Promotion Comes From God

The Psalmist tells us that the promotion of a man or his exaltation won't come from the east, west, north or south. In short, promotion doesn't come from anyone on earth. It comes from God above and God alone. We are created for expansion and growth. Our God is a God of progress — He progresses steadily in His work and plan. He wants us His children to also progress continually. He uplifts and promotes His people daily to higher heights in life. He said; "I want to make you the head and not the tail, to be above only and not beneath, and want you to lend to many nations and not have to borrow." Our God is the only One that can supernaturally promote you in a way that will baffle your detractors. The promotion that comes from God is the kind of promotion that defies human logic, and leaves people wondering how it happened.

After Joseph interpreted the dream of the Pharaoh and proffered his advice on how to contain the coming famine, the king said, "Since God has informed you of all this, there is no one so discerning and wise as you are. "You shall be over my house, and according to your command all my people shall do homage; only in the throne I will be greater than you." (See Genesis 41:39-40 NASB). Overnight, Joseph has gone from the prison to the palace, his circumstances changing suddenly and radically as he is "clothed in garments of fine linen" and decorated with "a gold chain around his neck." (See Genesis 41:41-43). He went from prisoner to Prime Minister of a foreign nation in one day! That is supernatural promotion, the promotion that comes from God.

As we can see, God's promotion can happen in an instant. One day Joseph is a prisoner, the next day he is a prince. This did not happen through manipulation or scheming on Joseph's part; it happens by the hand of God. God used a situation that should have led to his destruction as a means of promotion for him. God gave Joseph power to be victorious! Joseph overcame his fear of meeting his brothers. He overcame the stigma of his name. He overcame his past reputation.

144

He overcame evil. Why? Because at the prison in the midst of all his troubles he humbled himself, he held on to God and didn't let go.

You don't need to know any man before promotion can come to you. If God says you will not be promoted, you won't be. If He says you are qualified for promotion, no one can stop the promotion. The Bible tells us that "The king's heart is in the hand of the LORD; he directs it like a watercourse wherever he pleases." (See Proverbs 21:1 NIV) When it is time in God's sight for any man to move up, God will stir up the heart of those concerned, and it will be effected. Therefore, you must seek to please the Lord always. Because He is the One that commands promotion.

Beloved, some of the things fighting you are simply preparing you for where you are going. Your test and trials are the training grounds that God uses to prepare you for promotion. God loves you and is always using every circumstance you go through to move you closer to your promotion. In due season, you shall reap the promised harvest if you faint not!! God will promote you at His appointed time.

He said;

"Be still, and know that I am God. I will be exalted among the nations, I will be exalted in the earth!"

Psalm 46:10 (ESV)

As God is doing what He is doing in the earth and as you go from glory to glory, you go from different levels of wisdom, revelation, knowledge, anointing and understanding, remember God is a rewarder to those who diligently seek Him! Joseph's promotion came not from Pharaoh or his own hard work, but from the Lord rewarding Joseph's faithfulness. He literally went from prison to second in command simply by letting God use him. Joseph submitted to God's plan and God's process and thereby was right where God needed him to be so that he could be used for God's purpose.

We do not know how God is going to fulfill His promises in our lives, but one thing we can be assured is; IF GOD SAID IT, IT SHALL COME TO PASS! Now do your part and have unshakeable faith in the mighty name of Jesus!

Seeing the Unseen

"But without faith it is impossible to please him: for he that cometh to God must believe that he is, and that he is a rewarded of them that diligently seek him."

Hebrews 11:6

As Christians, we should never buckle under the pressures of life, but rather rise about any situation despite what it may look like with our human eyes. When you have great faith, no one will ever be able to convince you otherwise of something in which you believe is yours. The Bible says, "Now faith is the substance of things hoped for, the evidence of things not see. (Hebrews 11:1). Faith is belief with strong conviction; firm belief in something for which there may be no tangible proof; complete trust in or devotion to. Faith is not believing that God can but knowing that God will! Yes! Our God is still in the faith business.

The Apostle Paul said:

"The one who calls you is faithful, and he will do it."

1 Thessalonians 5:24

It is amazing how God can take a hopeless situation and turn it into a time of great rejoicing. Joseph's life was anything but peaceful.... Betrayed by his jealous brothers, falsely accused by his master's wife, thrown into prison and left to languish there for years. Yet when Joseph surveyed his circumstances, he was able to proclaim with boldness that what others meant for evil, God had used for good.

Some of the things fighting you are simply preparing you for where you are going.

Joseph acknowledges that even in the worst circumstances, God has worked in his life, that even through those who wished him harm God's mission to preserve the people has prevailed. He saw God as the "Great Engineer" behind even the worst of circumstances.

147

As we come to the fiftieth chapter of the book of Genesis, there are eleven grim faces staring down anxiously at the floor. All attention is focused on the man who is enthroned in front of them. They are huddled, these eleven are, before one of the most powerful rulers in the world, one who stands only behind Pharaoh in Egypt and he has the authority to execute them. He is dressed in fashion that would be fitting for one who had the position he had. He is the Prime Minister of Egypt; he looks down on these humble Jewish herdsmen as they stoop before him. He has had a long history with these men. It is a history of pain and suffering, and rejection, and the memories are vividly etched into his mind.

They had wronged him, this Prime Minister, in the past greatly. They had done great damage to him from a human perspective and now the tables are turned and he has the power and the authority and the ability to enact severe retribution against them. They are, in fact, his brothers who had betrayed him and the Prime Minister of Egypt is none other than Joseph, the one betrayed. You see, the Lord has a way of silencing our accuser! He has a way of bringing His people through difficult circumstances and situations.

When Joseph's brothers first came before him, he recognized them even though they didn't recognize him. It had been twenty-two years since they had sold him into slavery. They were much older and skinnier. They were in a place of desperate need. A famine had ravaged the land for two years, and Jacob had sent his sons to Egypt to buy grain. So they bowed down before Joseph, who was in charge of administering the grain, in a strange fulfillment of his childhood dream that he would rule over his brothers.

The question that is posed is that what is the action that Joseph will take against his brothers? Will Joseph take his revenge? When the silence is broken, it turns out that it is not anger, and it is not hostility. It is not threats. It is not statements of harsh punishment; it is rather the sound of weeping, crying. One by one as they lift their eyes and look at Joseph, he looks back and he looks back with a forgiving smile, tears stumbling down his face. His tears prove to be contagious and they all begin to weep. And we read the text, Genesis 50 verses 19 to 21.

Here are the words of Joseph;

"Do not be afraid for am I in the place of God? But as for you, you meant evil against me but God meant it for good in order to bring it about as it is this day to save many people alive. Now, therefore, do not be afraid, I will provide for you and your little ones. And he comforted them and spoke kindly to them."

There was no vengeance here. There was no hatred. There was no animosity. Joseph treated his brothers with mercy. He treated them with loving-kindness. He treated them with undeserved favor. But the question is this; How does kindness and love and mercy and grace become cultivated in the heart of one so wickedly treated? How does this attitude of complete forgiveness and compassion and affection and provision and comfort and kindness come out of the heart of one so horribly treated? The answer is found in what I call "Joseph's theology".

He had a clear understanding that what his brothers have done to him is evil. But though they meant it for evil, God meant it for good. He also had a clear understanding that God was at work and God is in control and you can trust God for the outcome. It was his theology of the sovereign purpose and providence of God that generated the attitude of his heart.

God says that He knows the thoughts that He thinks toward us, thoughts of peace, and not of evil, to give us an expected end! (See Jeremiah 29:11). God works His own ends, no matter what the intention of people be it good or bad, God will bring about His own ultimate end. And what God means to happen, will ultimately happen. He coordinates and organizes all the apparently independent activities, and thoughts, and ideas, and movements of people, pulls them all together, makes them harmonize with one another to effect His ultimate ends.

"For from him and through him and to him are all things.
To him be glory forever. Amen."

Romans 11:36 ESV

Brothers and sisters, unless you see the big picture of what God is doing through the difficulties of life, the suffering, the pain, the iniquities, the injustices of life, you will miss the profound and foundational truth that God is using all of it for your ultimate good and His glory.

> Joseph treated his brothers with mercy. He treated them with loving-kindness.

The big picture that Joseph saw was the reality that though they had mistreated him, it was in the purpose of God. And that purpose was so vast, and so all encompassing, and so far-reaching as really to be staggeringly amazing.

In fact, the Lord used Joseph's suffering and his subsequent circumstances to accomplish His own sovereign purposes. Far bigger picture! —God had a plan for the world and in order to fulfill that plan for the world, He had a plan for the nation Israel. And in order to fulfill the plan for the nation Israel, He had a plan for Joseph. And it all was tied together! What a Wonderful and Awesome God we serve!

Like Joseph, you may not always understand what is happening to you, but the Lord is always in control. He told me to tell you; "Don't let the facts change your faith! In this season of your life, everybody who didn't want you is now going to have to need you. Welcome to the season where the same people who looked

151

down on you will now have to look up at you!
Welcome to the season your haters are getting ready to
look at you in awe!"

Don't allow yourself to get lost in the seasons of
life, or to devalue today! Everything you are going
through is temporary. God is using those challenges to
prepare you for your tomorrow! To prepare you for
what He is doing now and what He will do. Don't
worry about your haters! The last place they left you
won't be the same place they find you. Joseph was left
in a pit but found in a palace. God is indeed up to
something great in your life. His Word encourages us
in the book of Jeremiah 29 that even if we walk
through the valley of the shadow of death, the Lord
God will be with us. He will turn our negative
backgrounds around to our favor in Jesus Mighty
name. Amen!

Believe! It's Turning Around For You!

God sees things we can't see. He understands
timing so much better than we do. He knows when it
is due season for our promotion and He knows who
all will benefit from it. He can put us in the right
places, at the right time, for the right purpose so that
His kingdom is advanced.

It is important to know that you can have an
assurance in God. The Bible says that He knows the
number of hairs on your head. He knows you better

152

than you know yourself. God knows what it will take to move, stimulate, activate, or motivate you. Ultimately He knows what it will take to get you into the place that He would have you. Therefore, He allows those unpleasant things; trials, storms to come in your life because He is just trying to perfect and direct you.

In 1 Peter 5:10 the Scripture says:

> *"But the God of all grace, who hath called us unto his eternal glory by Christ Jesus, after that ye have suffered a while, make you perfect, establish, strengthen, settle you".*

This verse makes it very clear about God plans toward His people. Yet, many Christians don't understand why things happen in their lives. Some of them in the past have had some very negative things and extremely hurtful things happen to them, leaving them wondering why would a God who is so just, loving, and kind allow such a thing to happen to them. But I want you to understand once again that God has a divine plan. He has a master plan for your life, but sometimes you may have to go through to get through.

> Like Joseph, you may not always understand what is happening to you, but the Lord is always in control.

153

Getting to the place where God ultimately wants you. It is also up to you to surrender to His will. Just like Jesus in the Garden of Gethsemane when He declared, "Nevertheless not my will, but yours, be done" (Luke 22:42).

Everybody goes through hard times once in a while. No one is exempt. However, as Christian we can rest assured that God will always be there in the moment of our crises. In Psalm 37:25-26 David said: "I was young and now I am old, yet I have never seen the righteous forsaken or their children begging bread. They are always generous and lend freely; their children will be a blessing." God's Word has given us many promises concerning His presence, His help in time of trouble, and His assurance that no matter what happens, we will become all we have potential to be.

From where Joseph stood there in that prison, his future may have begun to look a bit bleak, as if there was just no way out of his current circumstances. Sometimes, we too, can live through situations that seem so hopeless that it appears to be sheer foolishness to maintain a posture of faith, holding onto the notion that God is still able to do what we believe He will do. But God is able!

Able to do what, you ask? —Whatever He wants to do and He is well able to use whatever He wants in order to get you to where He wants you to be. The Word of God reminds us again and again that;

"All things work together for good to them that love God, to them who are the called according to his purpose."

Romans 8:28

In other words God takes everything in our lives; the good, the bad and the ugly, and works it all together so that the resulting outcome is actually "for our good". If you are going to trust God as you move through trials, tests and temptations in your life, you do well to remember that God is able to do exceeding abundantly above all that you ask or think, according to the power that worketh in you! And He is not done with you yet!

No matter what storm you are going through in your life, God has a way through it and above it. For believer, His strength will always be all that you need because He knew your name long before He formed the earth. The true God who knows all things loved you before you were born! He is in control of all of life! He is working in your life even when you cannot see His activity. He has a plan to deliver you and to promote you in His time.

If there is one thing you must remember about the covenant keeping God as you deal with "would-be-doubt-producing difficulties in life", it's that God is not done with you yet. In fact, He is never "done" with us. God is constantly planting, cultivating, growing and pruning His character in our lives as He methodically guides us from faith to faith and from

155

glory to glory. Your primary duty in all the situations and circumstances of life is to seek for ways to glorify Him even as you patiently wait for Him to accomplish His purposes in your life.

He has a plan to deliver you and to promote you in His time.

Beloved, you will have troubles but they are working in you a glory that will defy the enemy of your soul. You cannot lose in the mighty name of Jesus! The enemy can't take what was redeemed by Christ for you. Jesus has a way to help you and He will not fail. The troubles of this world cannot defeat you no matter how weary you become. No matter the situation, your future is bright!

When Jesus cried out on the cross, "It is finished", that was the promise shout of victory for those who believe in Him. The price was paid by the Blood of Jesus, and you are no longer in bondage to the evil of this world. Shame on satan! Thank God you are still here! You are going forward!

Each day is an opportunity to bring glory to God as you stand in faith trusting that He is with you in all things. Now, be strong and of good courage, do not fear nor be afraid of them; for the Lord your God, He is the One who goes with you. He will not leave you nor forsake you. Lift up your eyes for all that you need is with you today!

You can truly face tomorrow despite your pain because Jesus is with you. Let His peace be your comfort because He is working all things out for you now. You don't have to feel it or see it. You just have to know that His promises are real.

Here are the words of one of the songs on my album "Victory Noise" available online.... I pray that it encourages you.

Greater Is Coming

God is up to something new
Up to something great
I feel my breakthrough
I've got the victory
In Him all things are made new
The past is over now
I can shout, I can dance and praise His name
I know His plan is working
Everything out for my good
My God is up to something incredible
In the middle of the storm
I will lift my voice and praise
My God is up to something incredible
All I know greater is coming
Yes I know greater is coming

❖ ❖ ❖

"Your kingdom is an everlasting kingdom, and your dominion endures through all generations. The LORD is faithful to all his promises and loving toward all he has made. The LORD upholds all those who fall and lifts up all who are bowed down."

Psalm 145:13-14

157

Soul Nuggets

1. It is Gods will that we increase. It is His will that we increase in wisdom and knowledge, and that we prosper and multiply.
2. It is important to know that you can have an assurance in God.
3. Success in the Word of God is to be victorious; being able to overcome obstacles.
4. God takes everything in our lives; the good, the bad and the ugly, and works it all together so that the resulting outcome is actually "for our good".
5. The enemy can't take what was redeemed by Christ for you.
6. When Jesus cried out on the cross, "It is finished", that was the promise shout of victory for those who believe on Him.
7. You can truly face tomorrow despite your pain because Jesus is with you.
8. You don't have to feel it or see it. You just have to know that His promises are real.
9. You cannot lose!

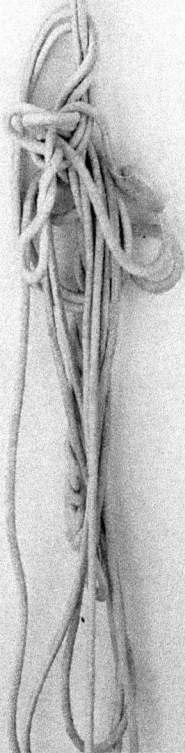

CONCLUSION

SAME GOD RIGHT NOW... SAME GOD BACK THEN

"I am still confident of this: I will see the goodness of the Lord in the land of the living."

Psalm 27:13

AT THE BEGINNING of this book, I share with you how I thought adversity would never come night my dwelling after I sold out to Jesus. As I said, it seemed the more I obeyed God the more adversity came my way. What strikes me the most is how God oftentimes takes the most painful experiences of adversity and uses them to prepare us for what lies ahead.

Beloved, problems of all sizes and degrees happen to everyone. When we come face-to-face with the problems, disasters, and tragedies of life, we need to remember God is in control. Why? Because if you don't truly believe that the Lord is in absolute control, you will suffer needlessly from fear and doubt, and you will inevitably have a wrong response to your problems. Then you will forfeit the blessings and rewards that God meant for you to reap.

The Scripture says:

"The Lord has established His throne in the heavens, and His sovereignty rules over all."

Psalm 103:19 (NASB)

What you have to realize and remember is that nothing can touch your life without God's permission. If He allows adversity, then He has a purpose for it— and it is always a good purpose. I have learned that since God is in control in every situation and circumstance, all I have to do is to get into agreement with His will and plans for me, and to follow His lead, and nothing can stop me from receiving His best. Even when others don't have good intentions for my life, I know that God does, and He will protect me if I look to Him for help.

God doesn't waste anything. Everything happens in our lives for a reason, and a great part of that reason is to help us grow in our faith. Even when evil people deliberately hurt us, God is in control! He doesn't always stop it, but He takes what they mean for our harm and turns it around for our benefit. He says:

> *"From eternity to eternity I am God. No one can oppose what I do. No one can reverse My actions."*

> **Isaiah 43:13 (NLT)**

When the Lord has a mind to work on your behalf, and you follow His lead, even the devil himself can't touch you. Our lives are in God's hand. If we are walking in fellowship with Him, then nothing can touch us unless it is allowed by God for our good. Proverbs 21:30 make us understand that, "There is no wisdom, no insight, no plan that can succeed against the LORD." The apostle Paul also declared, our God,

162

the blessed and only Ruler, is the King of kings and Lord of lords. (See 1 Timothy 6:15).

God is the Creator of the universe who yearns for you to know Him. That is why you are still here in spite of the storm and rain, heartache and pain. It is His desire that you rely on and experience His strength, love, justice, holiness and compassion. The Lord longs for you to believe with all your hearts that when trouble comes your way, He is in control! He is up to something great and good!

Brothers and sisters, the Lord's purposes will prevail! People can make plans, wise people can make plans, insightful people can make plans, haters can make their plans, but ultimately none will overcome the purposes and plans of the Lord about you! On this journey to your divine destination, you must walk by faith and not by sight. Even when it appears that evil people are "winning" or that their plans are succeeding, it is not reality!

> God doesn't waste anything. Everything happens in our lives for a reason, and a great part of that reason is to help us grow in our faith.

In reality, in view of all eternity (not the moment) God's plans cannot be stopped. He said: "I make known the end from the beginning, from ancient times, what is still to come. I

163

say: My purpose will stand, and I will do all that I please. From the East I summon a bird of prey; from a far-off land, a man to fulfill my purpose. What I have said, that will I bring about; what I have planned, that will I do." (Isaiah 46:10-11). Hallelujah!!! Glory be to our great God!

The One who knows what will happen tomorrow, next week, next year, the next decade. He is God and there is no one like Him! He knows what will happen in the world. More importantly, He knows what will occur in your life and can be there for you, if you have chosen to include Him in your life. He said; He can be "Your Refuge and Strength, an ever-present help in times of trouble." But you must make a sincere effort to seek Him. And if you will search for Him with all your heart, then you will find Him.

Today, I want to challenge you to decide right now to be determined and persistent in seeking God and being obedient to what He is telling you to do. Our enemy, satan, is persistent and will do whatever he can to wear us out and keep us from God's will. But we need to have the same tenacity in Christ to never give up! satan is not a gentleman, you can turn him down once but he doesn't care, he will come right back at you troubling you till you give in, and that is exactly what he tried with Joseph too.

I also challenge you to be strong in the Lord and don't let the opposition have the final word! Put on the whole armor of God! Get up each day knowing not only who you are, BUT whose you are. No obstacle

164

will hold you back! God knows what it takes to bring order back to your life. Trust Him and rejoice! He is working on something and everything around you will be made better.

The Best Is Yet To Come

When God puts a promise in your heart, don't be surprised if you face opposition. Don't be surprised if all kinds of adversity come against you. The Scripture tells us that the enemy comes immediately to try to steal the seed out of our hearts (see Matthew 13:19). He wants you to give up and think that God's promise is never going to happen. Remember Joseph's story, he was sold into slavery and he was mistreated, lied about, and forsaken. If anyone had a reason to give up, it would have been Joseph. He could have said, "God, I thought You put a dream in my heart. But I must not have heard right because the whole bottom has fallen out."

On the contrary, Joseph understood the principle that God is a God of completion, that He finishes what He starts. In the natural, Joseph didn't have any reason to be encouraged. He didn't have any reason to be positive and hopeful. But Joseph wasn't focused on the natural. He knew God was a Supernatural God! And in the end some thirteen years later, because he believed, because he stayed in faith, he saw God bring to completion exactly what He started in his life.

God wants to do the same thing for each one of us. He is saying to you today, " I am a God of completion. I finish what I start. If you will get your hopes up and start believing again, I will do for you what I did for Joseph. I will take what was meant for your harm and I will use it to your advantage."

Beloved, take God at His Word. Let His declarations be true and every other voice be silenced. Believe that no matter what has come against you, no matter how unfair it was, things are shifting in your favor. God still has a way to turn it around and bring to completion what He has put in your heart. Don't give up because your plans are seemingly put on hold or they are going in the opposite direction of your intended dreams because the best is yet to come!

> Take God at His Word. Let His declarations be true and every other voice be silenced.

If God could take Joseph from prison and set him on a throne in one day, will He not do the same for you? Is He the same God today that He was in Joseph's day? I believe He is, but the great question is this: Will you trust God in your prison as Joseph did in his? Are you willing to see your prison as a place to get to know God, rather than something to try to escape from? If you will really get to know God in your present circumstances, God can change those circumstances anytime He sees fit.

166

Conclusion

Today, you may not understand it all, but don't resist changes. You have to let go of the good and comfortable to have God's best. You must leave those things in God's hand, and set your attention on knowing and experiencing God's love where you are. Trust Him! He will do the rest!

Jesus said; "Let not your hearts be troubled, trust in God, trust also in Me." (John 14:1). Wherever you are at in life, or whatever it is you are doing, you must place your faith, hope and trust in God your Father and in Christ your Lord, for He guides you in paths of righteousness for His name's sake.' (See Psalm 23:3). And then whatever path He leads you down, whatever storm He leads you through, even if your dreams for the future are shattered in the process, you will respond by clinging to, relying on, and trusting in Him, instead of responding with shock, confusion and anger.

> You may not understand it all, but don't resist changes. You have to let go of the good and comfortable to have God's best.

Always remember what the Scriptures said about God's faithfulness to His Word. His promises are true and certain. He will never go back on His Word! Because He is faithful and a God of completion. He finished what He starts. Even if your situation, your dream, your marriage, your

167

children, are seemingly dead, God can still interject a BUT! Because He is the One who can revitalize dead dreams. Nothing is too hard for Him. So no matter who you are and no matter how dead your situation may seem, when God shows up, He can make the world's impossibilities a reality in your life!

As Joel Benson said: "Desperation is the breeding ground of miracles." God often places us in hopeless situations so that our desperation causes us to focus on no one but Him. If this is you today, if you are in a desperate situation, God can still turn your hopeless situation around. May I challenge you once again to do like Joseph and keep your eyes focused on the future.

Don't let your dream die because someone said, "You can't do it!"... "It will never come to pass!"... "You've messed up too many times!"...No! Believe God is a God of grace! He will turn your hardships into your blessings! —Yes, your situation might seem hopeless, beyond repair, and even impossible. But we serve a God that can turn hopeless situations around. We serve a God that specializes in our impossibilities! He is the only one who can take the good times, the bad times, and the ugly times we all endure and use them to instruct, strengthen, and refine us for His holy purposes.

Proverbs 3:6 says:

> *"In all your ways acknowledge him, and he will make your paths straight."*

168

Conclusion

Our God is sovereign over all things and He is untouchable. Nothing can match His Glory, strength, power, might, knowledge, blessings, riches, love, mercy, grace, omnipotence, agape Love, holiness, righteousness, forgiveness, omniscience, greatness, peace, joy, graciousness, gentleness, omnipresence, skill, handiwork, self-control, availability, sensitivity, patience, tenderness, kindness, faithfulness, goodness, humbleness, willingness, sympathy, empathy, beauty, strategic ways, consistency, intentionality, authority, and anything else you can possibly think of.

Our God is Awesome and Worthy to be praised. No matter what!

DEAR READER ALWAYS REMEMBER

Sometimes your plan B is God's plan A. God has the ability to take all the things of your life that seem to make no sense and use them all for His purpose and your benefit. In fact, He is going to use everything you have been through to get you ready for what He is going to do through your life! Like Joseph, God has planted seeds of greatness on the inside of you. He has predestined that those things in your heart come to pass. You may not see it, but you are a work in progress. God is ordering your steps, enlarging your territory and perfecting all that concerns you. Trust Him. Be encouraged. After the darkest days will come your biggest blessings if you remain faithful.

169

The best is yet to come! Just believe! What's coming is better than what is gone! If He did it before, He can do it again!!!

STAND FIRM AND BE BLESSED!!!

THOUGHTS & REFLECTIONS
❖ ❖ ❖

1. What do you do when God's timing
is taking too long?

_____

_____

_____

_____

_____

2. How do you understand God's plan
for your life?

_____

_____

_____

_____

_____

_____

_____

_____

_____

_____

3. What does it mean to you "Waiting on God"?

_____

_____

_____

_____

_____

_____

_____

_____

_____

_____

4. Read Genesis 39:8-9. What do you notice
about Joseph's answer to Mrs. Potiphar?
Why is it significant?

_____

_____

_____

_____

_____

_____

_____

_____

_____

_____

_____

5. What promises has God made you? Do you
expect that He will keep them? If so, how does
it change your approach to daily life?
If not, why not, and what would you do
differently if you did expect God to keep
His promises?

_____

_____

_____

_____

_____

_____

_____

_____

_____

_____

_____

_____

_____

6. As a believer, how can you overcome unforgiveness?

_____

_____

_____

_____

7. Why is God so interested in training or preparation?

_____

_____

_____

_____

_____

_____

8. What do you want God to accomplish through your life? How can you show God your gratefulness in advance for how He will work in your life?

_____

_____

_____

_____

_____

_____

_____

_____

9. Give 2 testimonies about God's faithfulness in your life.

_____

_____

_____

_____

_____

_____

_____

_____

_____

_____

_____

_____

_____

_____

_____

10. What are the things that you cannot see
    that you need assurance for today?

_____

_____

_____

_____

_____

_____

❖ ❖ ❖

ACKNOWLEDGMENTS

First and foremost, to my Lord and Savior Jesus Christ who has been with me in the pit and all the way to the palace! Thank You Lord for giving me the strength, wisdom, knowledge, and understanding to write this book!

To my precious wife Laetitia Bonsu and my two Princesses (Daughters); Janelle Kierra and Janessa Kimani Bonsu, I love you ladies very much. We have seen enough pits that we definitely do not want to go back there. Thank God for the Palace and together we are our way there.

I'm grateful to God for my Pastors; Yvan and Yves Castanou for obeying God in building ICC (Impact Centre Chrétien), the place that prepared me to reach God's people. Special thanks to Pastor Matthew Ashimolowo (for believing in me), Bishop Tudor Bismark, Bishop TD Jakes, Pastor Ransford Obeng, Bishop John Francis, Pastor Mensa Otabil, Pastor Prince David, Bishop Noel Jones…Also, special thank you to Nicolas "Nicky" Brown, Noel and Tanya Robinson. You guys are truly a blessing!

To my Parents, thank you so much for believing in me for truly "I have a Dream!... Not only do I have a dream, I have a Vision. Also to all of my family and friends, I love you all so much! You have always been there for me no matter what. You guys will forever be in my heart.

And finally, a Big thank you to all of the men and women of God who have had an impact on my life. May God increase you all!

ABOUT THE AUTHOR

Determined, Innovative, Anointed, and Cutting Edge are some words often used to describe JERRY BONSU. Founder and Senior minister of Victory Life International Center (VLIC), a revolutionary Movement of 'like minded' and 'like spirited' people coming together in one accord: whose mission is to empower and equip individuals through teaching and preaching the uncompromised Word of God, and helping them to fulfill their highest calling and usher them into a supernatural lifestyle of faith and abundant living.

Jerry Bonsu is a visionary leader who merges multimedia, the marketplace, and faith into one dynamic calling. He is also the visionary and founder behind several entities, including: Victory in Praise International Gathering, a vibrant, dynamic worship conference, which brings together more than 2000 people each gathering, — a wide audience of pastors, worship leaders, artists, musicians, scholars, students, and other interested worshipers. Founder and President of Jerry Bonsu Ministries (JBM); Jerry is also the leader of a gospel group Jerry Bonsu & Levitical Anointing; And the co-founder of a non-profit organization Elyon Foundation, created to influence the next generation.

Jerry — dynamic conference speaker, author, life coach, entrepreneur, worship leader... also travels throughout the world with his breakthrough teaching on understanding your God-given identity, purpose, and destiny in Christ. His mission is to impact his generation with divine revelation. Jerry and his wife, Laetitia are the proud parents of two children, Janelle Kierra and Janessa Kimani.

BOOKS & CD'S BY JERRY BONSU

* PUSH
(Praise, Pray, Persist Until Something Happens)

* The Path to Victory

* Dear Dreamer

* The Power Of I AM

* The Power Of I AM (Audio Book)

* I AM Who God Says I AM
(Biblical Affirmations Book & CD for Little Girls)

* I AM Who God Says I AM
(Biblical Affirmations Book & CD for Little Boys)

* Victory Noise (Album)

Order these inspiring products and more by visiting
www.jerrybonsu.org and be sure to join us on Facebook,
Twitter & Instagram for more inspirational words.

WWW.JERRYBONSU.ORG

PUSH

Praise,
Pray,
Persist
Until
Something
Happens

JERRY BONSU

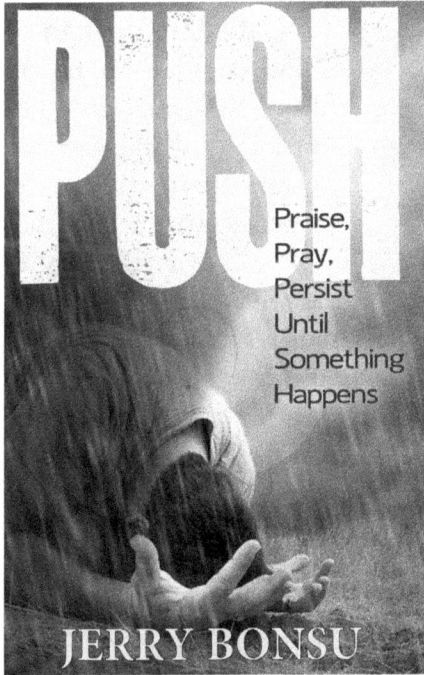

Believing that God can take you safely through all of the storms of this life can be difficult. God's timing doesn't always line up with our way of doing things and it may seem that we are alone in our battles. The raging storms of life brings many questions: What do you do when you are facing a serious medical issue, a crumbling marriage,

financial difficulty, an addiction or any overwhelming problem that just won't go away? How do you continue waiting on God especially when you are pregnant with purpose?

In PUSH, Jerry Bonsu shares practical truths about the power of Praise, Prayer and Persistence that will carry you to new and exciting heights of splendor, hope, and love that only the Master could design - especially for you. You'll gain insight into how you can learn to stand firmly and have lasting peace and confidence in the face of adversity.

THE PATH TO VICTORY

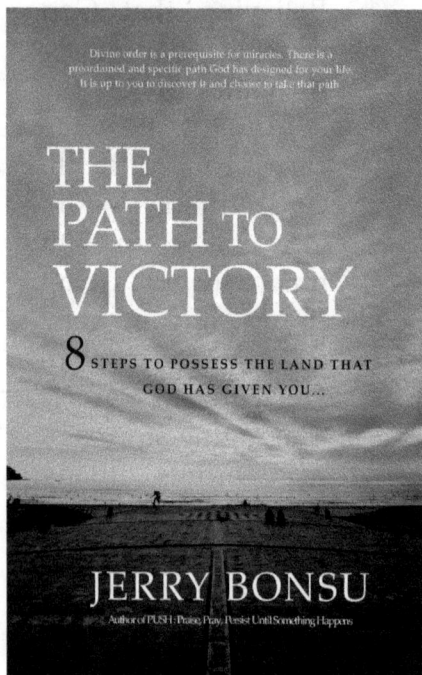

Divine order is a prerequisite for miracles. There is a
preordained and specific path God has designed for your life.
It is up to you to discover it and choose to take that path

THE
PATH TO
VICTORY

8 STEPS TO POSSESS THE LAND THAT
GOD HAS GIVEN YOU...

JERRY BONSU

Author of PUSH : Praise, Pray, Persist Until Something Happens

The Christian life is to be a life of victory in all things that pertain unto life and godliness. Even though there are many obstacles and trials that come our way that try to prevent us from walking in victory, we can experience the victory that God has ordained for us. God, the Father has introduced Himself to us His children as Jehovah Nissi, the one who gives us victory in all areas of life.

However many of us do not experience this victory because of the lack of some important foundational keys to empowerment. In this life-changing book « The Path to Victory », Jerry Bonsu gives clear, practical principles that will guide you step by step through the process you can take to possess your inheritance in Christ, achieve success, enrich your life, and discover your life's purpose.

DEAR DREAMER

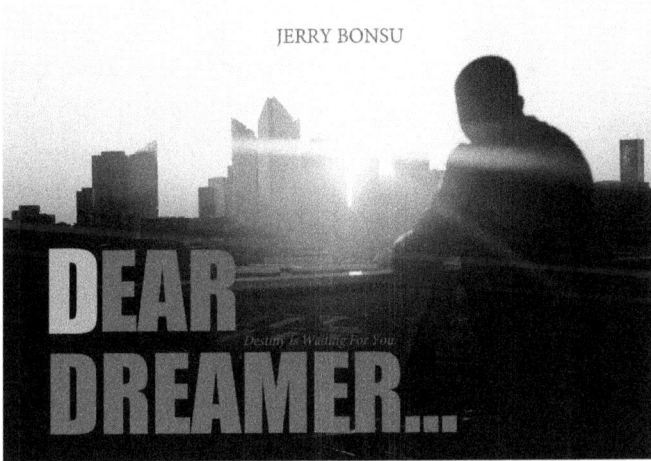

Dear Dreamer, What happened to the dreams that GOD gave you? Have you let your present reality determine your future reality? How long are you going to ignore YOUR dreams to help other people build theirs? Just like Joseph, your dream is the solution to someone's problem! What you have to offer is significant. Get your hopes up. Raise your expectations. This is exactly the moment to put your faith into action and expect God's blessings.

This book is a manual for those who are serious about fulfilling destiny and operating in purpose… this book is for you! I believe the hopeful messages and warm encouragement in this book will push you to expand your horizons beyond what you thought you were capable of doing so that you might go even further than you'd ever dreamed of going.

I AM WHO GOD SAYS I AM

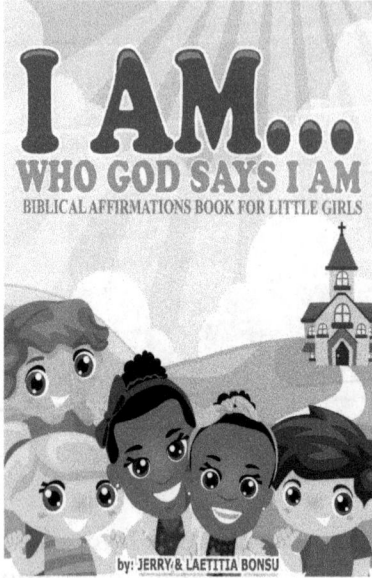

What This book consists of 26 Biblical affirmations based on the 26 letters of the alphabet. Each *affirmation is expressed* in a rhyme and is accompanied by a lovely illustration that is bound to delight your child and make you smile. There are so many "voices" in this world telling our kids they don't measure up. There are certain Biblical truths that your children should grow up knowing with absolute confidence.

Read "I AM Who God Says I AM" Biblical Affirmations for Little Girls; again and again with your daughter, granddaughter, niece or favorite godchild, and enhance your favorite little girls's self-image and promote her path to a bright and healthy emotional future. Jerry and Laetitia BONSU believes that you can change your world by changing your words... Remember, death and life are in the power of the tongue. That is why it is important to speak life (and not death) over your children and help them to declare God's words so that they can receive God's promises.

Is there a special little boy in your life? Grab "I AM Who God Says I AM" for Little Boys online or everywhere books are sold.

Also available in audio version

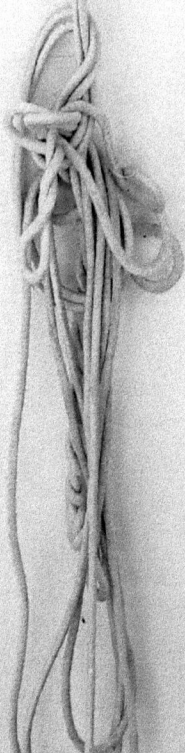

www.ingramcontent.com/pod-product-compliance
Lightning Source LLC
Chambersburg PA
CBHW070958040426
42443CB00007B/557